IAN BOTHAM
on FISHING

IAN BOTHAM *on* FISHING

WEIDENFELD & NICOLSON

Contents

On the Fly

Being Coarse

At Sea

'Give a man a fish and you feed him for a day.
Teach a man to fish and you feed him for a lifetime.'

Chinese proverb

'Give a man a fish to eat and you will have him for the evening.
Teach a man to fish and the weekend is yours.'

Old wives' tale

Introduction

This book I hope will be of interest to anyone interested in fishing of whatever type and of whatever level of expertise. For those coming to fishing for the first time I hope the blend of stories, information and humour will draw them in and for those already expert I hope it will give them food for thought – new experiences to try, new ideas about different ways, and places, to fish. For me, and for millions, I know, fishing is more than a hobby, it has become part of my life.

My first introduction to fishing was typical of many. From the ages of about ten to fifteen (after which cricket took over) I used to go down with friends to the River Yeo near Ilchester in Somerset and, like thousands of lads up and down the country, I caught a few Roach and Dace on traditional floats but I really didn't know what the hell I was doing. I didn't fish for about three or four years until I was reintroduced to it by my wife's parents, who went every year to Callander, in Scotland. They fished on the River Teith, which runs through the town, and is one of the best salmon rivers in central Scotland. I joined them one year and we stayed in some log cabins on Loch Lubnaig. I went into the fishing tackle shop in Callander, got myself a permit, went back up to watch a guy catching a couple of fish, caught the bug, and I've been fishing from that day on.

That guy catching fish was Willie Carmichael, and Willie and I have been friends ever since. Willie, together with Old Charlie Martin, taught me how to fish. Charlie was then ghillie for the waters of the Teith, and he taught me how to fish for salmon. I also learned the art of shrimping (which I know is banned on most rivers now, but there's one hell of an art to it), and how to worm. In those days it was predominantly spinning, worming or shrimping, and that's how it was done on the Teith. Willie Carmichael, amongst many things, also taught me the ancient art of tickling trout and other fish. He took me up to the spawning reeds, where the fish go to lay their eggs. The fish lie there, so preoccupied with what they're doing you can actually, very gently, stroke the side of a fish without them turning a hair. The biggest I've stroked was about 21 or 22 pounds I would guess, a salmon in a stream so small that I could straddle it.

After a few years of salmon fishing, I started to get interested in the mechanics of fly fishing, and now I rarely do anything else. Even if the guys I'm with say 'Oh well, the water's not right, its too high, spinning is probably better today', I'll still fly fish. I enjoy it; I love fly fishing, I think it's one of the most therapeutic things ever devised by and for man – and woman. And I really do believe that. They say every day that you spend fishing is another day added on to your life. For me, the fascination with fly fishing has something to do with running water, it's therapeutic I think – I don't seem to like the calm waters of lake fishing. I don't like sitting in boats, I like wading, I like being in the river or working the banks, because that's part of the river to me, it's about what's round the next corner. So I don't coarse fish now at all, but I suppose if I got into the finer techniques of fishing for carp and barbel or pike as some of my friends have, then maybe I would become more interested, but alas I haven't got the time. And when I do get the time to fish, I love to chase the salmon, the sea trout and the trout.

The ancient art of tickling trout. On the river Chess in Buckinghamshire, 1946.

'I enjoy the solitude of fishing, the peace of mind.
I much prefer getting out on the river on my own, just me
and the dog, fighting over the packed lunch…'

That's what its all about for me, it's all about the fly. Recently I visited
New Zealand to catch trout and, where most salmon fishermen would
be happy with an eight-pound salmon, I was getting eight-pound wild
trout on nine-foot rods. It was awesome fishing.

I'm happy fishing, end of story. If I'm fishing on my beloved Tyne,
which is just an hour away from home, I'm very happy with my own
company, and I think that's important because I have spent so much
time in the rat race, in the media eye in one shape or form or another.
I love being off on my own – once I get on the river I just lose track of
time. I can get into a pool that's a hundred yards long, and if I look at
my watch as I'm coming out the other end, it's probably three hours

*It's just me and my dog
Pinot… and a grilse – a
young salmon which has
spent one winter at sea.*

later – I've fished a hundred yards of water in three hours and it's gone in a flash. And when you fish, you are usually on your own anyway, even if you do go with someone else. If there are two of us, and we've got a beat a mile and a half long, we're not going to stand one behind the other, that would be bloody stupid. So you tend to split up, meet for lunch and compare notes. I enjoy the solitude of fishing, the peace of mind. I much prefer getting out on the river on my own, just me and the dog, fighting over the packed lunch…

How it used to be… serried ranks at the end of the day.

Fishing for me is not about catching fish; that's a bonus. If I'm going up to the Tyne in the summer, I'll get up at five in the morning, I'll be on the river, in the river, at seven, first light. I've never actually worked out why, because I never seem to catch anything at seven – the first bites are at about ten when it's warmed up, but that's not the point… I want to be there. It's just me and Pinot, my Jack Russell, who goes with me every-where when I'm fishing at home, and it's absolute tranquillity. It's peace, peace of mind, and as I say, time goes by without you noticing and you're completely relaxed.

I'm never disappointed with the fish I catch – I return them all any way. I suppose if they had any brain cells they'd just get on my line and be happy because they know they're safe. The amount of fish I ever kill you can count on one hand. The days have long gone, thank goodness, where you see pictures of rows and rows of salmon laid out on a river-bank. You used to walk into a hotel at the end of a day's fishing and see a dozen or more beautifully coloured hen fish that were about to spawn, oozing eggs. The late Jim Miller, whose sons Chris and Michael now run the Junction Beat on the Tweed and the Sprouston Beat below it, and various other bits of rivers, lectured me very early on in my fish-ing career that he didn't kill hen fish, ever, and he didn't kill a cock fish unless it was for him to cook and never to make up numbers. And that is a philosophy I abide by. I kill maybe three or four salmon a year for my family to eat, and that's it.

Most people who fish are pretty easy going and act the same way, but I've had the odd ghillie who I wouldn't rush back to be with again.

Above: *My favourite fly. I always use the Silver Stoat fly first before going on to try others.*

Following pages: *An early photograph of a tyro.*

They are few and far between now, as most ghillies have a genuine love of the river, and the environment in which they work. But I once had a ghillie who was more interested in killing fish: 'Oh, I can bang it on the head, and if you don't want it, sir, I'll give it to…'. I made it clear that I was paying for the fish and I didn't want to kill them. Anyway, we didn't fish together again. I apply the same principle to all the fish I catch. So I don't kill marlin either. The first thing I say to the boat crew is 'Look, lads, I don't care if it's a world record, I'm not killing it'. It's as simple as that – you can take photographs, you can guesstimate, but I will not kill any of the marlin we catch. Particularly as most of the big marlin, the ones over 500 pounds, are female, and the reason they're that size is because they've got a 400-pound egg pouch and that's for the generations to come.

Women are fishing in increasing numbers now. My wife Kath comes with me occasionally, as she did on a recent trip to New Zealand when she actually put waders on. Now you try getting most women into a pair of waders and wading boots… they are not exactly Versace! She put them on nonetheless and thoroughly enjoyed it. The scenery is spectacular; that's one of the enjoyable things about it. You don't very often fish in city centres. If you're looking for salmon and trout, you are usually in countryside, on your own, and usually with beautiful scenery around you. I've always said fishing will prolong my life; you're so relaxed and so chilled out at the end of a great day's fishing. On a river, things happen: you're in the water, it's running around you, there are fish moving, and bird and animal life to watch.

I remember, for example, fishing for Sea Trout and being stitched up by an otter. It was a memorable day fishing a pool with Gareth Edwards on the Towy, in Carmarthenshire in Wales, a wonderful river, and one of my favourites. The sea trout catches are bigger there than any other river in England and Wales. I nearly got hit on the head by a falling tree once but the fishing itself is just stunning. The water is beautifully clear and you can hear the sea trout sploshing around you… I was in a pool, fishing away and I had a good, strong pull the second or third cast, and then suddenly the line went slack. Then an otter swam up to me, he looked at me, I looked at him, he swam round me, and then he and his family were chomping on my sea trout

. . . he looks at me, I look at him, he swims round me, and then he and his family are chomping on my sea trout on the far bank . . .

on the far bank. And that was the end of fishing on the pool for that evening… That's what fishing is about!

As for kit, my essential fishing equipment is modest. When I know the river and know the fishing I travel quite light: two rods, I always take a spare just in case, waders (good waders – personally I don't like studs, I like felt on the sole), a jacket, and my Jack Russell, Pinot – he's an essential part of the kit. I carry a landing net, but I tend to beach the fish when I'm on my own, because you can control them better and release them more quickly so you're not putting the fish under any more stress than you have to. And glasses. I never, ever, fish without a hat and glasses, because I've had the experience of a hook ending up in my hat countless times. So anyone fishing, particularly fly fishing, please wear glasses. And preferably polarized glasses – you will need them anyway if you're stalking fish. A very good friend of mine had to drive for two hours to get help with a size 4 sea hook lodged in an eye. And you will need a good jacket because the weather changes, and a little rucksack – you will need a rucksack if you're on your own, with a few sandwiches in there to keep you going, and usually a bottle and some glasses. The Botham Merrill Willis Chardonnay kept in a cool jacket is a favourite – 'pleasingly buttery with a hint of oak', they say…

I mess around with flies, changing size more than colour. I'm convinced size is more important than the actual colour of the fly. I've noticed I'm slightly superstitious – I always use the Silver Stoat fly first. I tend to vary the size of the Silver Stoat before using other flies. But I've learned so much on my trips to New Zealand, like putting a nymph below your wet fly… it bloody works, though a lot of waters in the UK won't let you fish with two flies, so check first. But, if I'm absolutely honest, I catch ninety-nine per cent of the fish I get on Silver Stoat's Tails, but that's because ninety-nine per cent of the time that's what I fish with! So it's chicken and egg. I think the time of year dictates how you vary the flies. Towards the back end of the season you tend to use flies with reds and more distinctive colours. I think for summer fish, however, the black and silver just works. Then there is the Highland Glory… there are an amazing number of different flies, and I really do think it's right time, right place. It's the same for the guys who go spinning – one will tell you he will use a green and gold Toby, another a black and yellow Minnow, and when you ask questions you usually find it's what they caught their last fish with!

I've never tied my own flies; I'm colour blind, so it's a total waste of time. My son Liam tied a few flies for me a long time ago, but he hasn't done it for years. I get my flies from a magnificent fly tier, the Donegal Fishing Company in Ireland, and they tie the best bloody flies, and I could never compete with them. Their flies seem almost as if they're double tied. They last five or six times longer than any other fly I've used, and I don't mind giving them a plug because they are the best. So if anyone is looking to fill their fly box, go and have a look at the Donegal Fly Company first. Although I buy in my flies, I've developed a few knots, and one the boys teach you on the Spey is a fantastic knot for presenting the fly. And it's very simple. Mostly though, wherever you go in the world people use the same knots. Blood knots, the most commonly used knot, for example, are pretty much the same everywhere.

I've noticed a marked improvement in fishing waters after a period of decline – a lot of progress has been made in Britain. Take what's happened on my favourite river, the Tyne. Twenty-five years ago it was seriously polluted but it is now the best salmon fishery in England, and probably in the top six in the UK. They are magnificent salmon, always a good size – even Chris Tarrant caught one there. The river has come back to life because of the work and dedication of a number of people. Now I hear a rumour that someone is saying they don't need to keep the hatchery going any longer and that it should be shut down. I hope that's not the case, and I hope that we can keep the fishery going and can keep on improving it. Eliminating the pollu-

The golden mahseer of Southern Asia have been recorded at 9 feet in length and 18 pounds in weight. They are fierce fighters.

tion and stocking the river were the two factors in the Tweed coming alive again. Fishery maintenance needs strict rules: in New Zealand, for example, you cannot buy wild trout, only certified farmed fish, and only on certain waters can wild fish be kept –a and then only ones a certain size and then usually not more than one, sometimes two. So it is very strict. The result is that New Zealand fishing is, in my experience, the best in the world, simply because they look after it well.

The buying out of net fishermen has also made a massive difference to salmon fishing. There's still too much long lining, and there's still too much drift netting in various parts of the world. The Japanese are particularly bad.

Because of my job as a cricket commentator I travel a lot, so I get the opportunity to try out the fishing wherever I have to be. I've thoroughly enjoyed marlin fishing in the middle of nowhere on the Great Barrier Reef off Northern Queensland, Australia, which was stunning, and fishing for King George whiting in the seas off Melbourne. I don't like inland fishing in Australia because I have a snake phobia. I have fished in Tasmania at London Lakes, but that was fifteen or twenty minutes from Hobart by helicopter! The *Times* correspondent, John Woodcock, introduced me to bone fishing in the Windward Islands during the 1986 West Indies winter tour – I have an eight-pounder to my name, which is a pretty good bonefish. I've attempted permit fishing, but to no success whatsoever so far, because every time I go they disappear. I don't fish for shark – they should stay in the ocean. I don't mess with them, so that they don't mess with me, because they've got big teeth! The best trout fishing I've done in my life was in New Zealand. The biggest salmon I ever caught was a 28-pound Pacific salmon in the Waimamaku River outside Christchurch, though the best salmon fishing I've experienced has been in Scotland. But I haven't been to Norway or Russia yet, so until I have I don't think I'm in a position to say which is really the best and which isn't. I've been to

Three large Eurasian trout, or taimen (sometimes called river wolves because they hunt in packs) in the Eg River, Mongolia, photographed in 2007.

South Africa fishing for trout on the Berg River in Paarl, and Zimbabwe for bass on the fly, and for black spot bream and tiger fish in Lake Kariba. And I'm going to India this winter, to fish for mahseer. The mahseer in Himalayan rivers can reach seventy pounds and are recognized as fierce fighters. I tried going in 2007 but the river was flooded as they'd had unexpected rain. So I went on a tiger safari instead. I have a long wish list of places to visit. For example, I would like to go to Mongolia to fish for taimen, a giant, aggressive trout.

However, I do most of my fishing on rivers at home. The Towy in Wales is wonderful for sea trout, but so is the Esk on the Scottish border, a truly magnificent sea trout river. I've actually caught more sea trout on the border Esk than I have on the Towy, despite the latter's reputation. In fact, I haven't caught one on the Towy at all, but it's a lovely river to fish. I've had good sea trout on the Tyne, where you catch them during the day on the fly, which is unusual – and good sizes, too. I love spring fishing on the Spey, the topography of the place is beautiful, everything about it. I'm putting a new little syndicate together, there are five of us going up in April. I'm really looking forward to it. I love that fishing. It's not about the number of fish you catch, but if you get one, you don't forget it. Although I've done a bit of carp and pike fishing, river fishing for salmon, sea trout and trout is what I enjoy most. I love it, and I really get the same buzz stalking a ten ounce little wild Brownie in a chalk stream as I do chasing a 30-pound salmon. The joys of fishing…!

But my one wish yet to be granted is to find a remote river on the northern part of the Kola Peninsula, above Murmansk in Russia, as yet undiscovered by Western anglers. I know that in the Kola river itself anglers are regularly getting salmon of 20-30 pounds, and bigger. I'd love to explore those wild places and fish unknown rivers. The wilderness has a very strong attraction for me and to catch a salmon in such a river – well, it would be close to heaven.

In this book there is information about, and photographs of, places I go to regularly as well as places I want to try out. Sometimes I have written about my experiences of a particular place and the rods and lines and lures I like to use. But other sections offer alternatives according to the type of fishing, where you are fishing and a host of other variables. I hope the gives you inspiration and enjoyment. Happy fishing!

A Short (and Very Selective) History of Fishing

Above: *A halibut hook made at the end of the 18th century of wood and spruce root.*

Opposite: *An Egyptian fishing scene carved in limestone in the 6th century. The man on the left seems to be operating some kind of trawl net while the one on the right has a multi-hooked line with what appears to be bait below.*

Previous pages: *3rd-century Roman cupids fishing with rod and line in a fragment of a pavement from Constantine, in modern day Algeria.*

Spearing and, much later, netting were the earliest methods of choice for fishing according to the archaeological record. Dating the first use of a fishing hook is impossible as the earliest hooks were almost certainly made of perishable material such as shell, bone, horn and wood. We do know that fishing hooks made from the thorns of a hawthorn bush were used until relatively recently, and that native Americans used the claws and beaks of hawks and eagles to make hooks.

Straight bone hooks dating from 7–8,000 years ago have been found in Norway and one with a barb has been dated to 4,000 years ago. There are references to fishing in ancient Greek, Assyrian, Roman and Jewish writings, but some of the earliest detailed depictions of fishing methods using a hook and line are to be found in illustrations from ancient Egypt. Fresh and dried fish from the River Nile were a staple food for much of the population and various Egyptian implements and methods for fishing are clearly illustrated in tomb scenes, drawings and papyrus documents. Simple reed boats, woven nets, weir baskets made from willow branches, harpoons and hook and line (the hooks having a length of between one and seven inches) are all depicted. A Chinese account from around the 4th century BC also refers to fishing with a silk line, a hook made from a needle, and a bamboo rod, with cooked rice as bait.

Today, fishing, often called sport fishing to distinguish it from commercial fishing, is enormously popular all over the world, and in many countries it is the most popular participant sport. The problems of the modern angler are still the same as those that faced an ancient Egyptian on the banks of the Nile: where to find fish, how to approach them, and what sort of bait to use.

The history of angling is in large part the history of the tackle used, and its growing sophistication and efficacy. One of the earliest tools discovered is the predecessor of the fish hook, a gorge: a piece of wood,

Above: A Greek boy fishes with a rod and line around 500 BC. In the Roman era, as with so much of our knowledge of the detail of Roman life, pictorial evidence of fishing comes from mosaics that show fishing from boats with rod and line as well as nets.

Right: A 1st- or 2nd-century mosaic from Leptis Magna in Libya. Whilst one fisherman re-baits his hook the other plays a fish into his landing net. This is thought to be the first representation of a landing net and the pose is reminiscent of many modern photographs of the same scene.

bone, or stone an inch or so in length, pointed at both ends and secured off-centre to the line. The gorge was covered with some kind of bait. When a fish swallowed the gorge, a pull on the line wedged it across the gullet of the fish, allowing the catch to be pulled in. With the development of metal-working in the Bronze and Iron ages, the fishing hook was one of the first tools to be made. Initially it was attached to a hand line of animal or vegetable material, a method that was efficient only when used from a boat, but human ingenuity soon developed the practice of attaching the line to a primitive rod, probably a stick or tree branch, which made it possible to fish from the bank or shore. For thousands of years, the fishing rod remained short, not more than a few feet in length. The earliest reference to a longer, jointed rod is from Roman times, around the 4th century AD.

Fishing scenes are rarely represented in ancient Greek culture, a reflection of the lowly social status of fishing. However, there is a wine cup dating from 510–500 BC, now in the Museum of Fine Arts in Boston, that shows a boy crouched on a rock with a fishing rod in his right hand and a basket in his left. In the water below is a round basket-like object with a top opening, identified by archaeologists as a fish-cage used for keeping fish alive.

The Roman Claudius Aelianus, known as Aelian, who died in around 235 AD, has left us an astonishing body of work, full of detailed and unexpected glimpses into the Greco-Roman world, which includes a detailed description of fly fishing – specifically, of Macedonians catching trout using artificial flies with a six-foot rod and a line of the same length. The method used was therefore probably 'dapping': gently laying the bait on the surface of the water. Aelian also gives a detailed description of how each fly was made:

Above: *Barbed Roman hooks.*

Below: *A modern interpretation of the Macedonian fly, the 'Hippouros' fly described in Aelian's 3rd-century text, tied on a modern eyed hook. The original would have been tied on horsehair.*

'I have heard of a Macedonian way of catching fish, and it is this: between Borœa and Thessalonica runs a river called the Astrœus, and in it there are fish with speckled skins; what the natives of the country call them you had better ask the Macedonians. These fish feed upon a fly peculiar to the country, which hovers on the river. It is not like the flies found elsewhere, nor does it resemble a wasp in appearance, nor in shape would one justly describe it as a midge or a bee, yet it has something of each of these. In boldness it is like a fly, in size you might call it a midge, it imitates the colour of a wasp, and it hums like a bee. The natives generally call it the Hippouros. These flies seek their food over the river, but do not escape the observation of the fish swimming below. When then the fish observes a fly on the surface, it swims quietly up, afraid to stir the water above, lest it should scare away its prey; then coming up by its shadow, it opens its mouth gently and gulps down the fly, like a wolf carrying off a sheep from the fold or an eagle a goose from the farmyard; having done this it goes below the rippling water. Now though the fishermen know this, they do not use these flies at all for bait for fish; for if a man's hand touch them, they lose their natural colour, their wings wither, and they become unfit food for the fish. For this reason they have nothing to do with them, hating them for their bad character; but they have planned a snare for the fish, and get the better of them by their fisherman's craft. They fasten red (crimson red) wool around a hook, and fix onto the wool two feathers which grow under a cock's wattles, and which in colour are like wax. Their rod is six feet long, and their line is the same length. Then they throw their snare, and the fish, attracted and maddened by the colour, comes straight at it, thinking from the pretty sight to gain a dainty mouthful; when,

however, it opens its jaws, it is caught by the hook, and enjoys a bitter repast, a captive.' (Taken from *Radcliffe's Fishing from the Earliest Times*, John Murray, 1921.)

A Sea Fishing Revolution

Archaeologists studying the distribution and quantity of fishbones have pinpointed a time between 950 and 1050 AD as the period during which a fishing revolution occurred in Europe. A shift from freshwater fishing by individuals to extensive sea fishing began thanks to a combination of climate change, population growth, changes in religious practices and the increasing sophistication of boat making. The result was the opening up of trade routes throughout the Viking world to allow long-range trading of staples like dried cod – the beginnings of an industry that would flourish for a thousand years.

Viking tools found in Norway from the 6th century include a fish hook, a trident, a knife and various spear- and arrowheads, all beautifully functional.

The Art of Fishing Develops

There are scattered references in various writings that have survived from ancient times. In a poem written around 1060, a monk, Siegbert of Gembloux, mentions fishing on the Moselle with a hook, line and basket. In the mid-12th century, four Yorkshiremen were fined for poaching from a river with protected fishing rights. A German book written in the early 13th century by Wolfram von Eschenbach describes a man wading barefoot into a stream to catch trout and grayling using a 'feathered hook'. An early mention of fishing as a sport can be found in the writings of Giovanni Boccaccio, who recommended fishing as a diversion available to men of business and leisure in Florence in the mid-14th century. An early 15th-century book of fishing advice from the Bavarian abbey of Tegernsee lists at least fifty different fly patterns for catching carp, pike, catfish, salmon, trout and grayling as well as a startling recipe for bait involving the leg of a yellow frog steeped in urine and honey so that 'all fish will willingly bite on it in running and still waters'.

The known history of sport fishing in England began with the printing of the *Treatyse of Fysshynge wyth an Angle* (originally written in 1425 and printed in 1496) as a chapter in the *Book of St Albans*, in which the author compares angling to other field sports. Oddly enough, the essay was for centuries thought to have been written by an aristocratic nun, though this is doubtful. The work seems to have been based on earlier continental treatises dating back to the 14th century. With observations of insect life as a starting point, the author developed twelve different artificial fly patterns, one for each month, which are so well described that a modern fly tier could tie them without much trouble – and in fact, six of those twelve patterns are still in use today. Here is a description of how to make the Black Leaper, a fly to be used in May: 'The body of black wool and lapped about with the herl of the peacock's tail; and the wings of the red capon with a blue head'. What is groundbreaking is, firstly, the observation that a fish's choice of diet at certain times of year is dependent on the availability of insects and that therefore artificial flies should resemble the insects then swarming and, secondly, that catching fish is not the only benefit of fishing. 'A happy spirit' is mentioned as a consequence of fishing, brought on by a 'wholesome and pleasant walk', a 'sweet breath of the fragrant smell of the meadow flowers' and the 'melodious harmony of birds'. The author is equally knowledgeable about bait for coarse fish, and lists bait to be used in catching eighteen different kinds of fish, as well as where they can be found, or how they can be made, and how to breed live bait.

Fishing equipment in the 15th century was simple: tied flies, rods of ash, hazel or willow thought to have been up to about 15 feet long and jointed by metal links, with short lines of braided horsehair fixed to the top of the rod. Fish was important in the diet of the time, and the remains of fishponds can still be seen in the grounds of many large houses and religious institutions. Fish were often cooked in a pastry

Above: *The frontispiece to the 15th-century manual* Treatyse of Fysshynge wyth an Angle, *showing an angler using a six-foot rod with a horsehair line tied to the tip. In the Balkan mountains people still fish in exactly the same way today.*

Above: *A modern interpretation of a fly from the* Treatyse: *'The yellow colour in every clear water from September till November: for it is like the weeds and other types of grass which grow in the waters and rivers, when they are broken'. It is probably a mayfly imitation.*

Above: *Izaak Walton as depicted in the 19th-century edition of* The Compleat Angler, *edited by John Major.*

Above: *Fishermen of Walton's day with rods of 'five or six yards' from a 1760 edition of* The Compleat Angler.

case in the ashes of a fire and stuffed with a sweet and sour mix of breadcrumbs, sultanas, fruit, herbs and spices. Salmon did not have the status then that it has today, and was a common catch – so common that at the turn of the 15th century legislation was enacted that stated apprentices could not be fed salmon more than three times a week.

A 15th-Century Salmon Recipe

Take four ounces of white breadcrumbs, four ounces of apricots (roughly chopped), four ounces raisins, salt and pepper, one or two eggs to bind the stuffing, milk, and one teaspoon of dried mixed herbs. Mix all the ingredients together, but don't have it too wet or sticky. Push all this in the belly of a gutted salmon. To make the salt dough that encases the fish, mix together three pounds of flour, one pound of salt and some water. Roll it out. Put the fish in the middle and seal it up. Put it into a hot open fire until the pastry is black. Do not eat the pastry.

Fishing in the 17th Century

A great leap forward in technique came in the mid-17th century, which is reflected in Izaak Walton's classic *The Compleat Angler* (published first in 1653 and over the years in about four hundred new editions – five in his own lifetime – and in numerous languages). It is the first practical handbook of sport fishing, full of, as Walton says, 'the observations of the nature and breeding, and seasons, and catching of fish'. It describes not only the eating habits of many different fish and where to find them, but also what baits to use, as well as how to cook them. In 1676 it was expanded with a second section on fly fishing by his friend Charles Cotton.

The new section lists sixty-five trout flies complete with descriptions. Much development work had been done in the preceding century and many regional variations in fly patterns by then existed. Nonetheless, by its sheer popularity Charles Cotton's section in *The Compleat Angler* acted as a catalyst for the development of fly fishing for the next century and a half.

Fishing equipment in Cotton's time was still relatively simple, heavy and clumsy to operate: jointed rods were much as they had been a century before and lines were made of braided horsehair top-knotted in the absence of reels (which would make their first tentative appearance – known as 'winds' – in Britain in Cotton's lifetime). But hooks, made by needlemakers, were by then more durable as they were subjected to a hardening process. A combination of the plague and the Great Fire forced needlemakers to move out of London ,and Redditch in Worcestershire become a centre of needle and hookmaking. With industrialization came improvements in the quality of hooks, which became gradually thinner and lighter. Towards the end of the century wire loops made their first appearance on the tip end of rods.

Early Reels and Rods

The first winder, which appeared in the mid-17th century, was a rudimentary affair. It consisted of a wooden spool with a ring attached, through which the angler slotted a thumb. From the first appearance of a wire loop at the tip end of the rod the development of a rod in common use with a full set of line guides took about seventy years. By the 18th century, the fishing tackle trade had been firmly established, catering to the needs of a growing sport, and by the end of the century many fishermen were buying their flies rather than tying their own. In Britain the early 'Nottingham' reel based on the wooden bobbin used in the lace industry was the prototype for many subsequent designs. New machine-made tapered lines were being made which could be cast with greater accuracy than the old hand-woven horsehair.

Apart from the development of the multiplier (a reel with a free rotating spool which

Above: *Cotton's fishing lodge on the river Dove in Derbyshire where his and Izaak Walton's initials were placed above the door. 'It stands in a kind of peninsula, with a delicate clear river about it… I have in this very river that runs by us, in three or four hours taken thirty, five and thirty, and forty of the best trouts in the river.' It is here that Cotton took his friend, in the 1650s, as described in his additions to* The Compleat Angler, *to teach him fly fishing. They breakfasted on ale and a pipe of tobacco before the first lesson: he advised a rod of five or six yards should be long enough for a trout river – 'longer, though never so neatly and artificially made, it ought not to be, if you intend to fish at ease'.*

Left: *The river Dove.*

offered greater accuracy and distance when casting), reel design had barely altered since Walton's day. Early 19th-century reels were inadequate: the wide drum, narrow diameter reel continued to dominate the market. The British reels of this period that survive are of low quality. In America, a separate line of reel design was beginning to emerge. The majority of American reels were home-made affairs, having crude wooden spools with iron seats. In the early 19th century many Americans were still importing their reels, or making their own – discarded wool spools were often used, bound into frames by the local tinsmith.

Over the next hundred years reels, rods and lines became steadily more efficient, with the appearance of balanced crank handles, free-spool mechanisms, and shorter, lighter rods made of split bamboo, and with the replacement of horsehair lines with silk gut. The latter development was highly significant. The silk lines were easily cast, and with them the average angler could now cast three times further. Also, because they sank heavily if ungreased, or floated if greased, wet fly and dry fly fishing became possible. Developments to the Nottingham reel made it more free-spinning, which in turn made the reel revolve faster than the line was able to run off. This produced a tangled line (called an overrun in Britain, a backlash in the United States) and governors were devised to prevent this. A further refinement occurred at the end of the century when the level-wind, which automatically spread the line evenly as it was wound on the reel, was invented. In due course the fixed-spool reel or spinning reel became a standard in every tackle shop.

In the 20th century, developments took full advantage of the invention of new materials. Rods became shorter and lighter again, but still retained their strength as first fibreglass and then carbon fibre replaced traditional split bamboo. Nylon monofilament line and braided lines in other synthetic materials were developed and plastic coverings for fly lines allowed them to float or sink, doing away with laborious greasing.

The 1878 Act of Parliament for the Protection of Freshwater Fish
Known as the Mundella Act, this bill was sponsored by Anthony Mundella, Member of Parliament for Sheffield, and passed into law in 1878. Sheffield was a centre of coarse fishing and a number of angling societies, concerned by the potential decline of fish stocks by over-fishing, lobbied Mundella to sponsor an act proposing a general close season for freshwater fish to prevent gravid fish being killed in the breeding season. After a great deal of infighting amongst angling clubs and societies representing different interests, the bill became law and the very first case of fishing during a closed season was brought at Newark the following year when two defendants were fined the then large sum of five shillings.

Above: *A fly tied to gut. The problem with gut is that it has to be soaked before you can fish with it, and if it frays the fly attached to it is useless – you can't just tie on a new piece of line as you can with a modern hook eye.*

Left: *Silk lines, a brass reel and flies tied to gut. Silk lines required a great deal of care and were usually stored off the reel, after careful drying, to prevent them rotting.*

Right: *Waltonians Fishing Club, Sheffield, photographed on a club outing in 1897.*

Below: *Flies from Scrope's* Days and Nights of Salmon Fishing on the Tweed. *These are traditional Tweed flies with bushy bodies and teal, duck or turkey wings, materials which would be largely abandoned for the gaudy flies that followed. But these patterns work, as modern fly fishermen who have tried them attest.*

The Development of Salmon Fishing

The general notion that the salmon is king amongst fish is a relatively modern one. The 15th-century *Treatyse of Fysshynge wyth an Angle* mentions salmon fishing and Isaak Walton in the 17th century describes in *The Compleat Angler* a rudimentary fly reel for salmon, but it was not a prized fish in either period. Salmon fishing did not become a popular sport until the 19th century. Before that, salmon had been caught in nets or speared with tridents and either salted or packed in vinegar in barrels for wholesale markets. With the invention of ice packing salmon from the Spey in the late 1780s, the taste of fresh salmon became more widely known and prices rose. As gentlemen came north for long sporting holidays, they began increasingly to include angling with the more traditional pursuits of grouse shooting and deer stalking. One such was William Scrope, who wrote two books, one on the art of deerstalking, the other *Days and Nights of Salmon Fishing on the Tweed*, published in 1843, just as the craze for salmon fishing was taking off. It was however an Irishman, William Blacker, who made a profound impact on the sport of salmon fishing. Born in Ireland in 1814, he emigrated to England where he set up as a fly tier and general dealer in tackle. A traditionalist as far as his trout flies were concerned, it was his salmon flies that caused a sensation. His patterns

Flies from William Blacker's revised edition of The Art of Flymaking, 1855. These were among the first of the 'gaudy' salmon flies that swept away the traditional patterns that Scrope loved so much. They didn't work any better than Scrope's flies, but they caught more fishermen.

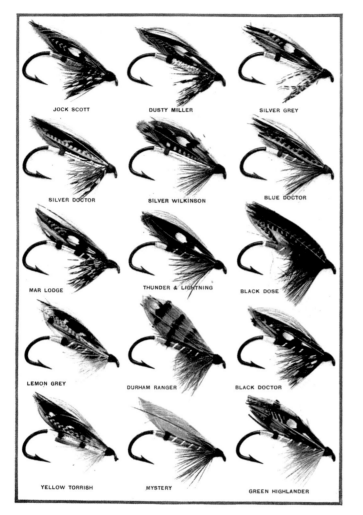

JOCK SCOTT — DUSTY MILLER — SILVER GREY

SILVER DOCTOR — SILVER WILKINSON — BLUE DOCTOR

MAR LODGE — THUNDER & LIGHTNING — BLACK DOSE

LEMON GREY — DURHAM RANGER — BLACK DOCTOR

YELLOW TORRISH — MYSTERY — GREEN HIGHLANDER

Above: A page from Ogden Smith's catalogue shows all the old favourites.

became hugely popular and so successful that he was able to charge large sums for tuition in fly tying. His *Blacker's Art of Fly Making, Comprising Angling & Dyeing of Colours with Engravings of Salmon & Trout Flies Shewing the Process of the Gentle Craft As Taught in the Pages. With Descriptions of Flies for the Season of the Year As They Come Out on the Water*, published first in 1842, became a classic of its time. A year after overseeing a new edition of his book Blacker died in 1856 of tuberculosis at the age of forty-two.

It was Blacker who was prominent among the tiers who blazed the trail for the so-called gaudy salmon flies in Britain, but it was very probably a compatriot called O'Shaugnessy, who flourished as a fly tier in Limerick at the beginning of the 19th century and whose colourful patterns became extremely popular, who was the catalyst. These gaudy 'Irish' flies percolated first into Scotland, and were noticed being used on the Tweed around 1810. They were so successful they quickly supplanted the duller, older patterns. Many elaborate but now classic salmon fly patterns still in use derive from that period, such as Thunder and Lightning, Silver Doctor and Black Doctor.

Before the mid century, anglers had fished with a small number of locally named flies regarded as suitable for a particular river. It was the development of the railways in mid-Victorian Britain that had a dramatic effect on the development of the salmon fly. Rivers fished largely by locals with their own store of local lore were overrun, particularly in

Scotland, with increasing numbers of fishermen from further afield, all anxious to try out the latest methods. The strong links which had existed between fly patterns and their rivers of origin began to weaken. But it was also true that when the new patterns were successfully used abroad in newly fashionable places like Norway, the potency of the link became a lost cause. By the end of the century there was a bewildering array of colourful patterns available, made from an astonishing variety of exotic materials proposed as suitable for any and every eventuality.

In North America experiments in fly tying veered away from the use of exotic feathers towards the use of hair from animals such as the bear, beaver, deer, fox or mink, first introduced in the 1890s. So complete is the revolution in fashion that the simpler hairwing as opposed to featherwing flies are now the fly of choice on the salmon rivers of the world.

The early 20th century heralded a period of innovation. A. H. E. Wood pioneered the technique of floating lines and floating flies for salmon in the years before the First World War, mainly on the Dee, which gained popularity in the 1920s. It was described in the

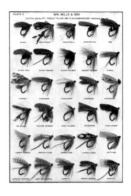

Above: *Trout flies on O'Shaughnessy-style hooks as offered by W. M. Mills, New York (established 1822) in their 1924 catalogue.*

Below: *A selection of vintage salmon flies with a mix of gut eyes and eyed hooks. All these patterns would be replaced by hairwing derivatives.*

Above: *A smallmouth bass taken with a deer-hair popper in Manitoba, Canada.*

Below: *The 'Dandy' rests on top of one of Jones's reels. It is tied with a gut eye rather than on an eyed hook, as came later.*

influential *Greased Line Fishing for Salmon*, 'compiled from the fishing papers of the late A. H. E. Wood' by Donald Rudd, first published in 1933. He observed that as water temperatures rose, salmon preferred to rise from the bottom of the river to take flies on, or close to, the surface. Previously, waterlogged silk lines had inevitably sunk, but with the greased-line system (Wood greased his lines with lanolin several times a day) the line floated. Presentation, Wood also decreed, was of the utmost importance, not just in the pared down fly itself, but how it was presented to the fish, drifting freely on the water. The fly should be presented '…in a natural manner; wobbling, rising and falling with the play of the eddies exactly as would an insect, or a little fish which was in trouble'. He wrote: 'I cast upstream so that the fly drifts downstream like a leaf'.

There were new developments in America at roughly the same time which, as knowledge of the life cycle of salmon increased, addressed increasingly technical issues. Lee Wulff became the most famous and knowledgeable pundit just before and after the Second World War with a string of books, films, articles and fishing camps where his discoveries became disseminated. He experimented with shorter rods and floating flies and the Wulff series of flies – the Gray, White and Royal Wulff – now form the backbone of many American tackle boxes.

Experiments continue. The tube fly is probably a North American invention, perhaps originating with Native Americans utilizing feather quills. Now plastic tubing is used. The advantages are that the size of hook can be changed at will as the hook is tied directly to the leader, which is threaded through the tube body as opposed to being integral with the fly.

The Development of Carp Fishing

Carp, the biggest freshwater species in Britain, was originally spread throughout Europe by monks between the 13th and 16th centuries to stock their 'piscinae' as a food stock. Only in the last thirty years has there been an explosion of interest in carp fishing for sport in the UK. In 1981 the Carp Society was formed and in just over twenty-five years has

Above: *A Grey Wulff fly.*

Left: *A photograph of Lee Wulff from his book The Atlantic Salmon published by the Winchester Press.*

become the largest specialist-angling organization in Europe. Carp fishing is now the largest and fastest growing sector of both coarse and game fishing, prompted in no small part by the sheer size the fish can attain. The current UK record is just over sixty-five pounds and the world record is eighty-nine pounds, caught in France in 2007. Many fisheries are dedicated to this one species and are highly managed and very profitable.

Before the 1970s it had been very much a minority interest. In 1895, 400 carp had been released into the Thames at Henley and for thirty years between 1925 and 1955 the Surrey Trout Farm had imported large amounts of fingerling Galician carp (king carp with enhanced growth through selective breeding) from a fish farm near Vassen in Holland. This resulted in good quality, disease-free stocks of carp being made available in the UK. The first really big carp in the UK was caught by Richard Walker, a forty-four-pounder in 1952 (called 'Clarissa') in the famous Redmire Pool, a three-acre farm pond in Herefordshire first stocked by the farmer with fifty small carp in 1934 to combat weed.

Given that a ten-pound carp has as much go in it as a twenty-pound salmon, it must have been quite a fight. Walker subsequently went on to be hugely influential in the development of stillwater trout fishing, and Clarissa spent the next twenty years in the London Zoo. Subsequently, Chris Yates caught a vast fifty-one-and-a-half-pound mirror carp on the same water.

The huge upsurge in the popularity of carp fishing in the early 1970s and the pursuit of the largest specimens resulted in big fish being legally imported to the UK from Continental Europe to create instant big carp waters. Many died from disease and for a while the practice was halted. But by the 1980s unscrupulous operators were once more importing big fish illegally. Concern for the welfare of the fish and the ecosystems in which they were being kept was the catalyst for the formation of the 'English Carp Liberation Army', a name which many regarded as perhaps too radical – the Carp Heritage Organisation (ECHO) took over in 2001, dedicated to educating people about the threats posed to existing aquatic environments by both regulated and unregulated fish movement.

There is a growing concern that the huge rise in commercial fisheries in lakes, gravel pits and ponds where large fish are stocked and fed is

Above: *Robert Walker with the famous 44-pound carp Clarissa he caught in Redmire Pool* (right) *in 1952*

having a deleterious effect on fishing as a whole. The *Times* fishing correspondent Brian Clarke raised the issue in his column in 2005: 'Signs are emerging', he wrote, 'that easily reached, customer-friendly and instantly gratifying stillwaters are taking anglers away from rivers. Consistent success on rivers is hard won: it takes effort and knowledge and tactical skills – and it cannot be guaranteed. One of angling's appeals is its sheer unpredictability… the angler rarely knows when a bite is coming or what species and size of fish may result. When a net full of fish is taken or a whopper is landed, the elation and sense of achievement are real… Heavily stocked commercial fisheries, with their guarantees of success, do away with all of this. And over time, it seems reasonable to ask, if there are no blank days and problems to be overcome – what then?... if monsters are regularly landed not because they are hard won but because only monsters are stocked in that place, from whence comes the sense of achievement and how can interest be sustained?'

A number of organizations and societies with substantial memberships have grown up over time and now organize and oversee much of Britain's carp fishing. The sheer scale of current interest in carp fishing is underlined by a recent Environment Agency telephone survey which recorded that over half of licence holders stated carp as their preferred quarry.

In the US, by contrast, the introduction of carp was not for the benefit of the leisure fisherman but to bolster food stocks. In the 19th century native North American fish such as basses, sunfish, crappies, pike, walleye, perch, trout, sturgeon, freshwater drum, buffalo fish, catfish, suckers, bullheads and others, were viewed as a natural resource and were harvested commercially. They were shipped by rail to markets where they were an important food source for a growing population. But an expanding population required larger harvests and stocks of

Dieter Markus Steiner with the then world record carp, weighing 84 pounds, in Germany, 2006. In October of the following year Paul Meredith caught an 89-pound leviathan at La Graviers in France. The same fish had also been caught the previous year, then weighing 83 pounds.

lake and river fish began to decline. The US Fish Commission was convened in 1871 to oversee the nation's fisheries and amongst its first tasks was to consider what species to introduce to bolster food supplies. In 1874 it issued a report entitled 'Fishes Especially Worthy of Cultivation', which concluded that no other species except the carp promised so great a return in limited waters. Its good qualities were cited as: it could 'attain large weight kept in small ponds and tanks', had high fecundity, was adaptable to artificial propagation and to environmental conditions unfavorable to equally palatable species, rapid and hardy growth, was harmless in relation to fish of other species, was able to populate waters to its greatest extent, and had fine table qualities, adding 'there is no reason why time should be lost with less proved fishes'. Three hundred and forty-five scaled, mirror and leather carp were duly imported from German suppliers. They were placed in ponds in Maryland and some were transferred later to the Babcock lakes in Washington, DC.

In 1879 some six thousand fingerlings were produced in the Babcock Lakes and were shipped to 273 applicants in twenty-four states. About the same number were produced in the Baltimore ponds. The following year over thirty thousand were shipped to 1,374 applicants. The rise in production and distribution was almost exponential and during the years 1879–96 the US Fish Commission distributed 2.4 million carp, some of which were sent abroad to Canada, Costa Rica, Ecuador and Mexico. By 1897 the Commission discontinued propagation and stocking because carp had been distributed virtually everywhere. The states took over and were involved in the propagation and stocking of millions of carp in hundreds of lakes and rivers. In terms of introducing a food resource it had been an outstanding success. Commercial harvesting started in the early 1900s and declined only in the years following the Second World War when ocean fish took over at a time when the oceans were perceived as pure and rivers were becoming polluted.

As a result of this massive effort to install carp from coast to coast, generations of American anglers have had the opportunity to enjoy carp as a sport or food fish. In some quarters, particularly in Australia, because of its sheer abundance, it is classified as a pest.

Fishing in North America

There are sporadic mentions of fishing in documents dating from the early years of colonization, but most are to do with the serious business of fish as a source of protein for those carving out a new world. As a sport, as opposed to a necessity, fishing became established only towards the end of the eighteenth century, and a few hardy souls went into business to supply the necessary materials and equipment.
The separation of fly fishing from bait fishing as an 'art' in its own right in the minds of certain anglers took hold in the mid-19th century, almost exclusively in the eastern states, and a debate raged for the next fifty years as to which fish should be given the status of 'game' and which 'rough' or 'coarse'. An edition, adapted for the American market, of Walton and Cotton's *The Compleat Angler* appeared in 1847.

In 1850 William Herbert's *Fish and Fishing of the United States and British Provinces of North America* (Herbert was of English origin and

The first US edition of Walton and Cotton's The Compleat Angler *with copious notes by George Bethune, published in New York in 1847. The old spike-foot reel propping the pages open would have been old fashioned even in 1847. The spike was pushed through a hole in the butt of the rod and the thumbscrew tightened on the lozenge-shaped washer to keep it firmly in place.*

Above: *A cane rod used with a centerpin reel – a traditional carp fishing setup.*

Right: *a fifteen-inch brown trout photographed just after release.*

Below right: *A beautiful little brook trout in the Catskill rivers.*

adopted the name 'Frank Forester' to sound more authentically American) offered the definition of game fish as 'those that take the natural or artificial bait and which would have sufficient rigor, courage and velocity to offer such resistance and give such difficulty to the captor, as render pursuit exciting'. Note that for Herbert the debate was about the nature of the fish and not the means of securing it. The mid-19th century saw the introduction of the first split-cane rods (invented by a fishing violin-maker) and in due course they began to be mass-produced. They were superior to the rods in use in Britain – much lighter and with a better cast – and by the end of the century began to be used extensively abroad.

In the last quarter of the century the popularity of the sport took off. The *American Angler* was founded in 1881, the first publication devoted entirely to fishing, and *Field and Stream* began in 1896. In 1893 the state of Minnesota, alarmed by the floods of anglers attracted to its burgeoning waters catching large numbers of fish by any practical means, was the first to impose numerical limits on fish catches. Four years later *Fly-Fishing and Fly-Making* by John L. I. Keene was published, surprising Europeans by showing how far the sport had developed in the US. Handily adjacent to the city of New York, the Catskill rivers such as the Neversink and the Beaverkill became the American equivalent of the classic chalk streams of Hampshire.

But American rivers were on the whole different to the more placid waters of Britain, and the controversy that raged amongst the purists at the dawn of the 20th century was about the merits of dry versus wet flies. Emlyn Gill addressed the controversy in his *Practical Dry Fly Fishing*, published in 1912. He noted that fishing with a dry fly as a lure was practically universal in England, 'that home of scientific sport', and that conversely the wet fly was the more used in North America. The picture painted of the ultra purist makes amusing reading today. He introduces his readers to the concept of 'fishing the stream' (wet) and 'fishing the rise' (dry). The English dry fly purist casts only when he sees a trout rising and does not make another cast until he sees another rise. If he sees no rises, then there are no casts, and he 'does not wet his line'. But fishing the rise requires relatively calm water to observe the ripples of rising fish, not the generally turbulent streams of the United States where the fisherman casts instead to where, by local knowledge, he knows the trout live and hide and seek their food. But Gill observed that because 'armies of fishermen are constantly delving into trout streams the fish become after a while so wary that any fly that does not pretty exactly counterfeit the real thing fails to attract their notice'.

In Europe the brown trout was the prime target for most fly fishermen. In the USA it was the brook trout in the eastern states, the

Casting at brown trout feeding on nymphs in a section of river that is open all year.

steelhead or cutthroat in the west. But constant delving of 'armies of fishermen' had seriously depleted the supply of brook trout and trout of various kinds began to be imported from Europe.

The first, brown trout, came from Germany and became known as 'German trout' (the same year the Germans received a shipment of rainbow trout from the US). The traditional method of fishing the stream, or downstream wet fly fishing, began to be ineffective against these new, more wily species and the focus turned to English methods of dry fly fishing and a range of experts developed indigenous methods suitable for local use. Theodore Gordon, who settled on the Neversink, was one who began to tie wet and dry flies to imitate local insects and went on to create many classic and original patterns, the best known being the Quill Gordon. Gradually a range of different patterns of bucktails (hairwing flies) and streamers (featherwing flies) in imitation of fish fry of different species and in different stages became widely used.

George LaBranche perfected a technique for overcoming the problem that Gill had so eloquently written about, how to fish effectively with dry flies in relatively rapid streams. His *The Dry Fly and Fast Water*, published in 1914, made American dry fly fishing really popular. His

influential contemporary Edward R. Hewitt categorized the development of fly fishing into three phases: first, the aim was to catch as many fish as possible; then came an interest in catching as big a fish as possible, of whatever type – and with that came a growing interest in records; and, more recently, a focus on particular species of fish which present a challenge to catch.

Hewitt was of the school that the presentation of the fly was all-important. A fly box groaning with a wide variety of flies in his view should be discarded in favour of a much smaller number correctly presented. He and another writer, James Leisenring, basing their theories on intensive observations of insect life on the water, did much to popularize nymph fishing. As always, with such different conditions and temperature variants over such a large landmass, there was a willingness to experiment with a wide variety of lures, techniques and equipment, in marked contrast to the more fixed assumptions prevalent in the British Isles and Ireland. Bass fishing, for example, travelled from the east coast with the westward expansion of the railways. Bass, it was discovered, could travel unharmed for several days in barrels, and largemouth bass were released in farm ponds and reservoirs across the country whilst smallmouth bass were introduced to rivers and streams. In the south in particular, largemouth bass multiplied quickly in the warm water and soon reached large sizes. In the east, as trout stocks declined due to overfishing and damming of rivers (causing them to rise in temperature) smallmouth bass took over as the fish of choice for sport fishing. In an encyclopaedia of 1881 the bass is described as 'a fierce biter, and, unlike the trout is not a timid fish. He is particularly fond of romantic streams and dilapidated mill-dams'. With the popularity of bass fishing soaring, the 20th century saw the creation of specific rods, reels and other necessary equipment.

It was in the development of big game sea-fishing in particular that that the US was to lead the world. In 1898 near Santa Catalina, an island off the Californian coast, a Dr Holder landed a 183-pound blue fin tuna on a rod and reel from an open skiff. He had battled the fish for three hours and forty-five minutes and in that period it was estimated that his boat was towed more than ten miles. He had gone to Santa Catalina because of the sheer density of fish in the waters there. He also witnessed the wasteful slaughter of fish. He was 'amazed and horrified at the sight of men fishing with landlines from the beach, pulling twenty-five to thirty-five pound yellowtail as fast as they were cast .. a depressing sight as most of these fish were thrown to the sea lions and sharks'. Inspired by his capture of such a large fish with a rod and reel and appalled by 'the unsportsmanlike conditions of fishing the island' (by handliners), he proposed the organization of the Tuna Club, of Avalon, Santa Catalina, the world's first game fishing club, to be formed 'for the protection of the game fishes of Southern California'. The concept of sportsmanship in angling was promoted and subsequently fishing rules and ethics were codified. The rest, as they say, is history.

Fishing Today

As with so many sports developed and codified by the British, anglers carried their traditions overseas and Australia, New Zealand, India and parts of Africa and North America have all developed their own thriving home-grown techniques based on local conditions. The British didn't only carry their traditions overseas, very often they also carried

Top: *Angling for tuna from a small boat off Santa Catalina, California at the end of the 19th century,* and bottom, *weighing a big sea bass caught in the same way. Both photographs were published in Charles F. Holder's* Sport Fishing in California and Florida.

An Edwardian gentleman trophy fishing in the days before catch and release.

the fish themselves. In 1864 the ova of salmon and trout reached Tasmania unscathed, and the oldest fish-rearing facility in the southern hemisphere can still be seen today in the Derwent Valley of Southern Tasmania. Thirty years later, a shipment of rainbow trout reached Australia from the US, another having already been dispatched to New Zealand a decade earlier. As a result of this piscatorial imperialism rainbow or brown trout have left their mark in almost all the appropriate habitats in every corner of the world.

The countries of Scandinavia, too, were popularized by British fishing tourists in the 19th century and went on to develop and establish themselves as popular destinations. With the growth of air travel in the last quarter of the 20th century almost every country in the world became accessible to anglers. The growth in charter boats equipped with sonar made the open seas around the continental shelf a play-

A pike in a landing net before release.

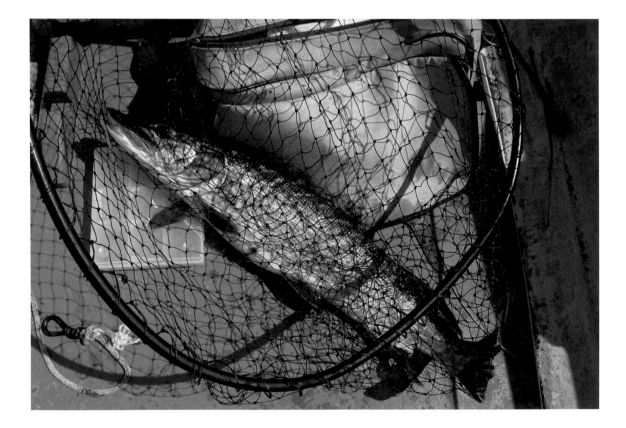

ground for big game fishermen. The giant black marlin of Australia's Great Barrier Reef spawned a new generation of fishing boats big enough to live aboard.

Hewitt's categories continue to be refined, these days with an emphasis on developing techniques to make the sport ever more challenging, including using lighter tackle, in certain circumstances using the fly for both saltwater and freshwater fishing. And new species of fish have come on the menu, too: the dorado of Argentina, the tigerfish of Central Africa, the bonefish native to shallow coastal waters, and the barramundi of Australia. With the demolition of the Iron Curtain, Russia and the countries of Eastern Europe have also welcomed anglers and many Westerners have been surprised to note that carp, considered a pest in North American waters, and given no credence as a source of food in Britain, is regarded as a delicacy and fished for widely in this part of the world. And bass fishing has become so popular in the United States that it has become an industry in its own right.

New introductions to Britain have increased the possibilities for freshwater anglers. Pike are now being fished in a number of highland lochs specifically for sporting purposes (a pike of over forty-seven pounds has been caught in Loch Lomond) and grayling have been introduced in several Scottish rivers to provide year-round angling. Roach shoals have proliferated in the lower reaches of the Clyde, Forth and Tay rivers (and tench have spread throughout the Forth and Clyde canal after small scale introductions in the late 1960s), and the opening up of bream, tench and rudd waters has greatly expanded the number of coarse fishing clubs. The last twenty years have seen a rise in the popularity of barbel fishing and related support groups. Some introductions have not been beneficial. The Eurasian ruffe, a small spiny perch, has been infiltrating waters in Britain and the US. Aggressive, with a capacity for explosive growth (a female can lay between 45,000-90,000 eggs a year) and a tendency to eat fish eggs, it could prove a potential threat to native fish stocks. But perhaps the most profound recent change, in the light of dwindling fish stocks, has been the catch-and-return policy now promoted by almost all fishing organizations and adhered to by so many individual anglers.

Freshwater Fish Identification Guide

Atlantic salmon

Atlantic Salmon (Fly)
Salmo salar

Distribution
Atlantic

Habitat
Anadromous, or ocean-going species, returning to their native freshwater rivers and streams to spawn. Can live entirely in freshwater. These are called Ouananiche or Sebago.

Appearance
Silver body with steel-blue spots on the flesh. Distinct narrowing at the root of the tail.

Diet
Omniverous

Barbel (Coarse)
Barbus barbus

Distribution
Europe

Habitat
Found on the bottom of the middle reaches of moderately flowing low-land rivers. Common where the river bed is gravely and in weir pools. Usually most active at night, largely in schools.

Appearance
Long and muscular dark brown or grey body fading to a light under-side and reddish-tinged fins. Two pairs of barbules on the side of the mouth help locate food.

Diet
Omniverous

Note: An especially prized sub-species is found in Spain called the **Spanish Barbel.**

Barbel

Barramundi

Barramundi (Coarse/Sea)
Lates calcarifer

Distribution
Indo-Pacific

Habitat
Catadromous, migrates from freshwater to the sea to spawn. Found in rivers, creeks and mangrove estuaries. An especially prized sporting catch in Queensland, Australia.

Appearance
Similar to the freshwater Perch. Greenish-bronze body fading to silver sides and white underside. 'Barramundi' is derived from an Aboriginal term meaning 'large scales'.

Diet
Piscivorous, also crustaceans

Bream (Coarse)
Abramis brama

Distribution
Europe and Asia

Habitat
Favours deep slow moving rivers, backwaters, reservoirs and flooded gravel pits. Found in schools close to the bottom and moves into shallow waters to feed.

Appearance
Deep-bodied with a narrow profile and protruding upper jaw. Larger bream have a dark bronze body fading to an almost black underside Silver bream are smaller with lighter coloured fins.

Diet
Almost exclusively tiny *chironomid larvae*, commonly known as bloodworm.

Brown Trout (Fly)
Salmo trutta

Distribution
Worldwide and heavily cultivated

Bream

Brown trout

Habitat
Common in artificial still waters, reservoirs, lakes and some rivers. Thrives in cooler temperatures and cleaner waters.

Appearance
Dark brown body with small spots of various shades of red and blue. Large mouth full of sharp teeth.

Diet
Piscivorous, also invertebrates.

Chub (Coarse/Fly)
Squalius cephalus

Distribution
Europe and Asia

Habitat
Generally found in clean and fast-flowing rivers. Favour gravel or stony beds. Continues to thrive in winter.

Appearance
Dark green body with amber or silver flanks. Rounded head and large mouth. Convex reddish anal fin.

Diet
Piscivorous, also small invertebrates and *caddis larvae*.

Common Carp (Coarse)
Cyprinus carpio

Distribution
Worldwide

Habitat
Large lakes and slow flowing rivers in lowland areas.

Appearance
Deep, stocky body. Colouration ranges from dark brown to grey. Two pairs of distinctive barbules around the lips.

Diet
Omniverous, primarily small invertebrates.

Chub

Crucian Carp (Coarse)
Carassius carassius

Distribution
Europe and Asia

Habitat
Large lakes and slow flowing rivers in lowland areas. Also found in shallow ponds. Shelters in muddy beds during winter.

Appearance
Varied colouration, generally dark green body, golden flanks, and reddish fins. Well-rounded head with no barbules.

Diet
Mainly zooplankton, fauna and water plants.

Carp

Dace (Coarse/Fly)
Leuciscus leuciscus

Distribution
Northern Europe and Asia

Habitat
Middle reaches of rivers and upstream brooks. Less often in slow-flowing lowland rivers. Prefers to move in shoals.

Appearance
Slim body with silver flanks and grey fins. Similar to the chub but with a smaller mouth and concave anal fin.

Diet
Small invertebrates, particularly *caddis larvae*.

Eel (Coarse)
Anguilla anguilla

Distribution
Europe, but all European eels are thought to spawn in the Sargasso Sea.

Habitat
Catadromous, breeding in the sea and migrating to European fresh-

Eel

Dace

Perch

waters. Buried in mud or lying near the banks of fresh water lakes and lower river estuaries. Very solitary.

Appearance
Distinctive sinuous shape. Dark black or grey body though some develop a yellow-tinged underside. Protruding lower jaw and large eyes.

Diet
Piscivorous, also terrestrial and aquatic worms, other invertebrates and plant matter.

European Perch (Coarse)
Perca fluviatilis

Distribution
Northern Europe

Habitat
Lowland lakes and slow flowing rivers. Sometimes found in still water. Moves in schools when younger, becoming more solitary with age.

Appearance
Dark green body marked with vertical stripes and reddish fins. Sharp spines along dorsal fin and pointed edges around gill covers.

Diet
Piscivorous, occasionally cannibalistic.

Note: The similar **Yellow Perch** (*Perca flavescens*) is found in the United States. Native to Africa, the giant **Nile Perch** (*Lates niloticus*) is a highly sought-after catch.

Golden Mahseer (Game)
Tor putitora

Distribution
Asia

Habitat
Found in streams and lakes. Favours rapid moving waters with rocky bottom. Tends to move downriver.

Appearance
Sap-green-coloured body with large bright golden scales. Ferocious set of teeth.

Diet
Omnivorous

Grayling (Coarse/Fly)
Thymallus thymallus

Distribution
Europe

Habitat
Favours clean and cool rivers. Thrives in well-oxygenated water. Also found in natural lakes, often in mountainous regions.

Appearance
Steely blue body with violet stripes fading to silvery flanks. Distinctive 'sail-like' dorsal fin extending along a third of its length.

Diet
Mainly insects, nymphs, small worms and crustaceans.

Gudgeon (Coarse)
Gobio gobio

Distribution
Europe and Asia

Habitat
Bottom living in lakes and rivers, usually in slow flowing areas. Found in some stillwaters. Most abundant were there are gravel bottoms.

Appearance
Small but sturdy brown-green body fading to silver-yellow sides with dark purple markings on the flank. A pair of short barbules around the mouth.

Diet
Bottom-dwelling shelled invertebrates, *caddis larvae* and small aquatic worms.

Grayling

Largemouth black bass

Largemouth Black Bass
(Coarse/Fly)
Micropterus salmoides

Distribution
Europe and the Americas

Habitat
Prefers clear and relatively warm waters. Favours areas lush with vegetation. Found in estuaries, rivers, lakes and ponds.

Appearance
Greenish-brown body fading to yellow-white underside. Darker coloured jagged horizontal stripe on the flanks. Large mouth.

Diet
Piscivorous, also water birds, small mammals and baby alligators.

Gudgeon

Northern Pike (Coarse)
Esox lucius

Distribution
Northern Hemisphere

Habitat
Lakes and slow flowing rivers or canals. Adults prefer deep water and areas with lush vegetation.

Appearance
Mottled green body with distinctive oval-shaped spots on the sides. Razor sharp teeth.

Diet
Piscivorous, occasionally cannibalistic as juveniles.

Note: Native to Asia, the **Amur Pike** (*Esox reichertii*) is prized by anglers.

Rainbow Trout (Game)
Oncorhynchus mykiss

Distribution
Worldwide, bar Antarctica

Rainbow trout

Pike

Habitat
Artificial still waters, reservoirs, lakes and some rivers. Favours fast-flowing water for breeding. Can thrive in warmer and murkier waters than the brown trout.

Appearance
Elongated silver body, occasionally metallic pink around the eyes. Heavily spotted, especially around the tail.

Diet
Omnivorous; occasionally cannibalistic.

Note: The **steelhead** is exactly the same species but is sea-going. Native to tributaries of the Pacific in Asia and North America, they are generally larger than the rainbow trout.

Roach (Coarse)
Rutilus rutilus

Distribution
Europe

Habitat
Lowland lakes, slow flowing and deep fast-flowing rivers.

Roach

Tench

Rudd

Particularly common where there is good weed growth. Prefers muddier waters.

Appearance
Very similar to the Rudd. Silvery-blue body with orange coloured fins and a white underside. A striking red-orange iris.

Diet
Omnivorous

Rudd (Coarse)
Scardinius erythrophthalmus

Distribution
Europe and Asia

Habitat
Oxbows and backwaters of large lowland rivers, canals and lakes but has been widely introduced to less typical waters. Thrives in heavily weeded and less-oxygenated waters.

Appearance
Dark green body with orange coloured fins and a white under-side. Protuding lower lip aids surface feeding. Golden iris.

Diet
Omnivorous

Tench (Coarse)
Tinca tinca

Distribution
Europe and Asia

Habitat
Largely found in lakes, canals and pools, sometimes lower reaches of rivers. Can tolerate warm waters. Prefers areas thick with weeds and vegetation.

Appearance
Short and stocky dark green to black body. Short pair of barbules on the upper lip.

Wels catfish

Favours dark areas with overhanging vegetation.

Appearance
Mottled dark-green to black body. Without scales. Six distinctive barbules around the mouth.

Diet
Piscivorous, occasionally shellfish, crustaceans, amphibians and wild fowl.

Tiny scales, rounded fins and a sharp, almost forked tail.

Diet
Bottom-dwelling invertebrates and insect larvae.

Wels Catfish (Coarse)
Silurus glanis

Distribution
Europe and Asia

Habitat
Slow flowing lowland rivers and still waters. Largely nocturnal.

Zander (Coarse)
Stizostedion lucioperca

Distribution
Europe and Asia

Habitat
Prevalent in the middle reaches of lowland rivers and larger still waters. Most active in twilight conditions.

Appearance
Resembles a hybrid of the Pike and the Perch. Pointed head with a very large eye and ferocious teeth for hunting. Spikes along the dorsal fins.

Diet
Almost exclusively piscivorous.

Zander

Saltwater Fish Identification Guide

Atlantic cod

Atlantic Cod
Gadus morhua

Distribution
North Atlantic

Habitat
Very varied, including rocks, reefs, wrecks, coastline, harbour walls. Occasionally form schools.

Appearance
Browny-green body fading to silver on the underside. Upper jaw extends over the lower. Single bar- bule protrudes from the lower jaw.

Diet
Omnivorous

Atlantic Mackerel
Scomber scombrus

Distribution
North Atlantic

Habitat
Migrates in large numbers forming large schools near the surface. Moves inshore in spring.

Appearance
Silver body with dark blue-green striped markings. Large mouth and eyes. A streamlined shape aids fast swimming.

Diet
Omniverous, but particularly plankton.

Atlantic mackerel

Ballan wrasse

Bluefin Tuna
Thunnus Thynnus

Distribution
Atlantic and Pacific

Habitat
Temperate and subtropical waters. Highly migratory and only occasionally ventures inshore.

Appearance
Dark blue body fading to grey. Large mouth, conical-shaped head.

Diet
Piscivorous, also crustaceans.

Ballan Wrasse
Labrus bergylta

Distribution
Eastern Atlantic

Habitat
Very shallow waters, up to 70 feet deep. Prefer rocky or weedy areas Occasionally found on offshore reefs.

Appearance
Coloration varies and includes browns, greens and reds. Prominent protruding lips and very strong, flat-shaped teeth.

Diet
Shellfish, invertebrates, occasionally small fish.

Blue Marlin
Makaira nigricans

Distribution
Atlantic, Pacific and Indian Oceans

Habitat
Tropical and temperate waters, appear to prefer bluer waters. Prevalent in the Gulf of Mexico.

Appearance
Blue-black body with a silvery-white underside and cobalt striped markings. Spear-shaped upper jaw snares prey.

Diet
Piscivorous, as well as octopus and squid.

Bluefin tuna

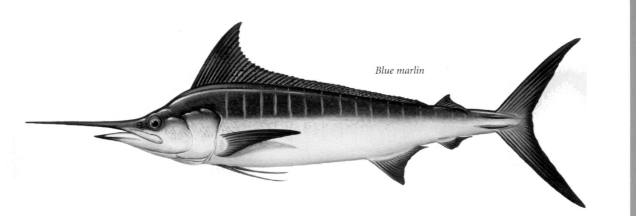

Blue marlin

Blue Shark
Prionace glauca

Distribution
Worldwide

Habitat
Prevalent in temperate and tropical waters and tend to follow the Gulf Stream. Prefer deeper waters, moving inshore as temperatures rise.

Appearance
Slim deep blue body fading to a white underside. Big eyes, a conical snout and large pectoral fins.

Diet
Almost exclusively piscivorous. Occasionally sea birds.

Brill
Scophthalmus rhombus

Distribution
North Atlantic, Mediterranean and Baltic Sea

Habitat
Prefer deeper offshore waters. Usually found on sandy beds. Can camouflage themselves to hunt.

Appearance
Flat rounded brown-green body with mottled markings and a light pinkish underside.

Diet
Smaller crustaceans, occasionally small fish.

Blue shark

Skate

Coalfish
Pollachius virens

Distribution
Northeastern Atlantic

Habitat
Found in inshore and offshore waters at depths of up to 1,000 feet. Move to coastal waters in spring.

Appearance
Very similar to the pollack. Olive green body fading to a silvery grey underside. Single small barbule protrudes from the lower jaw.

Diet
Pisciverous, also small crustaceans.

Coalfish

Bull Huss
Scyliorhinus stellaris

Distribution
Northeastern Atlantic

Habitat
Found both inshore and offshore and prefer rough, rocky seabeds.

Appearance
A member of the dogfish family. Sandy body with dark mottled markings that aid camouflage. Two distinct nasal lobes.

Diet
Bottom-living invertebrates.

Common Skate
Dipturus batis

Distribution
Eastern Atlantic, Western Mediterranean and Eastern Baltic Sea.

Habitat
Bottom-dwelling. Prefer deeper waters.

Appearance
Lightly spotted olive-green/brown-grey body fading to blue-grey underside. Very long and pointed snout. A row of twelve to eighteen spines runs along the tail.

Diet
Bottom-dwelling invertebrates and fish, as well as lobster, crab and other smaller rays.

Dab

Conger Eel
Conger conger

Distribution
Eastern Atlantic, Mediterranean and Black Sea

Habitat
Favours rocky ground, often around reefs and wrecks. Adults found in deeper waters close to the seabed.

Appearance
Coloration varies according to habitat. Strong jaw with ferocious teeth. Without scales.

Diet
Omnivorous nocturnal hunter.

Dab
Limanda limanda

Distribution
Northern Europe

Habitat
Prefer clean sandy or muddy beds, usually in shallow inshore waters. Occasionally found on rougher shingle patches. A common catch for shore fishermen.

Appearance
Light brown body, irregular dark markings and a white underside. Distinctly curved lateral line rising over the pectoral fin. Can camouflage themselves to hunt.

Diet
Predominantly crustaceans but also small fish, molluscs and worms.

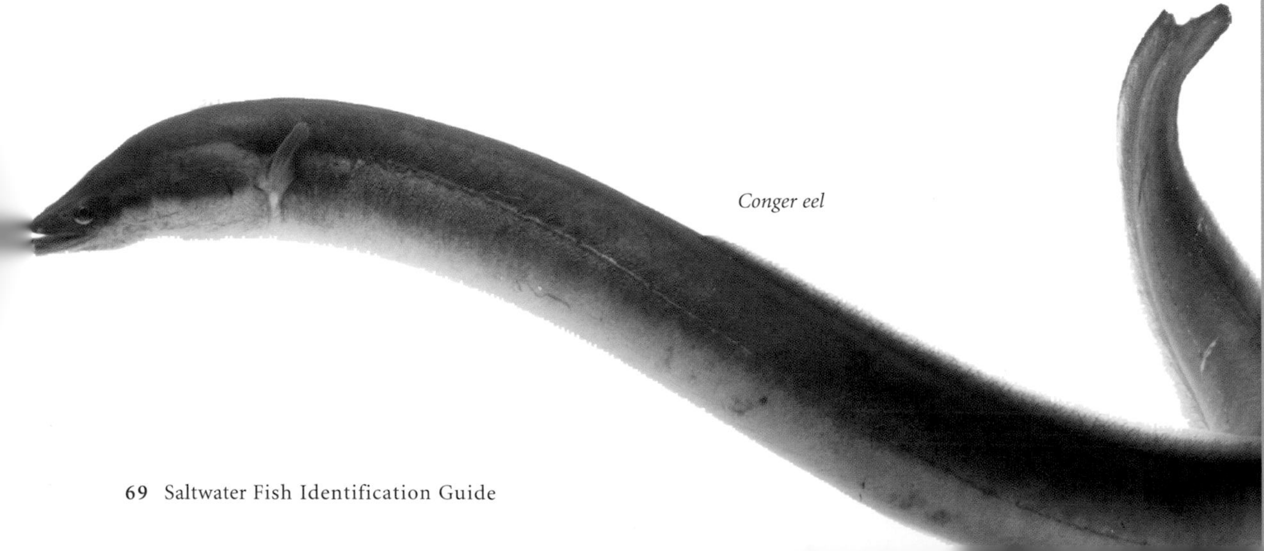

Conger eel

European plaice

European Flounder
Platchthys flesus

Distribution
Northern Europe

Habitat
Coastal waters, often just a few inches deep, but they can venture further. In colder climates sometimes found in freshwater river estuaries far from the sea.

Appearance
Deep bodied with a narrow profile, irregular reddish spots and a white underside. Can camouflage themselves to hunt.

Diet
Invertebrates, occasionally small fish.

European flounder

European Plaice
Pleuronectes platessa

Distribution
Across Europe

Habitat
Shallow water fish, though move deeper as they age. Lurks on gravel or sandy bottoms as well as mussel beds.

Appearance
Brown body with large red orange dots. A bony ridge behind the eyes. Smooth scales.

Diet
Invertebrates, especially small crustaceans, molluscs and worms.

European Sea Bass
Dicentrarchus labrax

Distribution
North Atlantic

Habitat
Predominantly saltwater but occasionally enter brackish or freshwater. Thrive in warmer waters and congregate around rocky coasts.

Appearance
Elongated body with dark silver flanks fading to a white underside. Two sharp dorsal fins.

Diet
Pisciverous, also invertebrates.

European Turbot
Psetta maximus

Distribution
Northeastern Atlantic, Mediterranean, Baltic Sea

Habitat
Shallow waters with sandy or rocky seabeds. Also common in brackish water.

Appearance
Almost circular, disc-shaped dark mottled body. Can camouflage themselves to hunt.

Diet
Other bottom-living fish, crustaceans.

European turbot

Garfish
Belone belone

Distribution
Worldwide

Habitat
Surface-dwelling, prefer warmer waters. Often found in large shoals and follows similar migratory pattern to mackerel. Most often caught near to the shore where they come to hunt.

Appearance
Bright green-blue body and light underside. Horizontal silver band on the flanks. Needle-shaped 'bill' or 'beak' on the lower jaw.

Diet
Very small fish and zooplankton.

Sea bass

Garfish

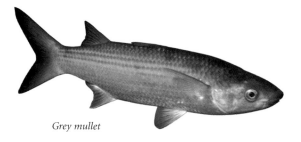

Grey mullet

Grey Mullet
Mugil cephalus

Distribution
Worldwide

Habitat
Calm waters around islands, near rivers and estuaries. Prefer sandy or muddy beds in salt, brackish and freshwater. Spawn in saltwater.

Appearance
Olive-green to grey body fading to silver with a white underside. Short pectoral fins and a large 'V' shaped tail. Large eyes.

Diet
Zooplankton and algae

Note: Similar species include the **thick-lipped grey mullet** *(Chelon labrosus)*, **thin-lipped grey mullet** *(Liza ramada)*, and **golden grey mullet** *(Mugil auratus risso)*.

Haddock
Melanogrammus aeglefinus

Distribution
Northern Hemisphere

Habitat
Favour deep waters, up to 1,000 feet. Prefer sandy or muddy bottoms. Migrate seasonally.

Appearance
Grey body with a white underside Striking black spot above and behind the pectoral fin. Big eyes and short, round nose.

Diet
Small invertebrates

Haddock

Lesser Spotted Dogfish
Scyliorhinus canicula

Distribution
Northeastern Atlantic, Mediterranean

Habitat
Bottom dwelling. Prefer sandy, coral type structures, mud and rocky areas. Found in very shallow waters up to depths of around 350 feet.

Pollack

Appearance
Member of the shark family. Light brown body with dark and occasionally light spots. Extremely rough skin that should be handled with care.

Diet
Invertebrates and slower bottom-dwelling fish.

Appearance
Member of the Cod family. Long body, dark brown to grey body. Single long barbule protrudes from the middle of the jaw.

Diet
Piscivorous, occasionally invertebrates.

Lesser spotted dogfish

Pollack
Pollachius pollachius

Distribution
North Atlantic

Ling
Molva molva

Distribution
Northern Hemisphere

Habitat
Found in very deep waters. Prefers areas with substantial rock formations or even wrecks.

Habitat
Larger adults favour deeper waters Fond of wrecks and reefs. Smaller pollack stay found around pier walls and other rocky marks.

Appearance
Member of the cod family. Dark green to bronze body fading to a lighter underside. Small scales and large mouth with a protruding bottom lip.

Diet
Invertebrates, occasionally small fish.

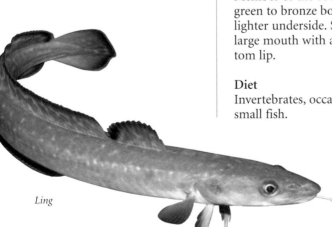

Ling

Pouting

Pouting
Trisopterus luscus

Distribution
Eastern Atlantic and Western Mediterranean

Habitat
Inshore waters around 350 feet deep, although have been found at 1,000 feet. Smaller pouting favour shallows, larger ones tend toward rocky substrates and wrecks. Sometimes travel in shoals.

Appearance
Dark brown body fading to a white underside. Pinkish tinged flanks with darker vertical bands and a black spot at the base of the pectoral fin. Large eyes and a single barbule in the middle of the jaw.

Diet
Invertebrates, occasionally small fish.

Red Sea Bream
Pagellus bogaraveo

Distribution
Northeastern Atlantic

Habitat
Prefers rocky and weedy areas. Can be found in waters up to 800 feet deep. Move in shoals.

Appearance
Orange tinted body fading to silver underside. Prominent scales and a twelve-spined dorsal fin.

Diet
Small fish, occasionally invertebrates.

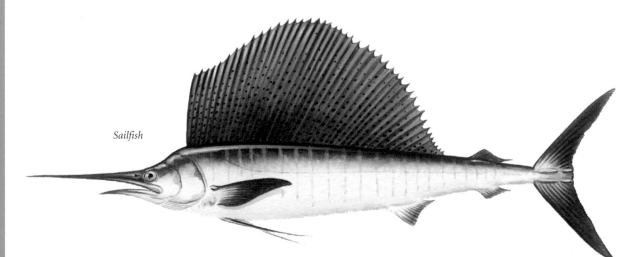

Sailfish

Sea bream

Black Sea Bream
Spondyliosom cantharus

Distribution
Eastern Atlantic, Mediterranean and Black Sea

Habitat
Favours rocky or weedy ground and also reefs and wrecks. Prefer deep water and forms shoals.

Appearance
Flat blue-gray body fading to silver and white underside, often with dark vertical markings. Prominent scales and an eleven-spined dorsal fin.

Diet
Invertebrates, occasionally small fish.

Sailfish
Istiophorus

Distribution
Atlantic *(Istiophorus albicans)*. Indo-Pacific *(Istiophorus platypterus)*.

Habitat
Prefers tropical and temperate waters, migrating towards warmer inshore waters. Occasionally form schools. Surface, mid-water and reef edge feeders.

Appearance
Dark blue body fading to a white underside. First dorsal fin is black spotted and resembles a sail. Spear-like bill similar to the swordfish and the marlin.

Diet
The fastest fish in the sea, a successful predator and almost exclusively piscivorous.

Sole
Solea solea

Distribution
Eastern Atlantic, Mediterranean Sea

Habitat
Prefers warmer waters, usually at depths of less than 150 feet. Move to deeper waters up to 500 feet in winter. Usually caught close to the shore in shallow, sandy waters.

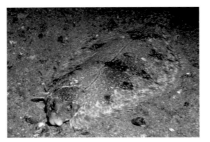

Lemon sole

Thornback ray

able coloration, though always deeply mottled. Prickly upper side.

Diet
Bottom-feeder, especially crustaceans.

Tope/School Shark
Galeorhinus galeus

Distribution
Atlantic, Pacific and Indian Oceans

Habitat
Found in inshore and offshore temperate to tropical waters. Highly migratory.

Appearance
Grey body fading to a white underside. Long pointed snout. Small razor sharp teeth.

Diet
Piscivorous, also crustaceans.

Appearance
Oval-shaped dark brown body with large dark spots. Rounded head and hook-shaped mouth. Camouflage themselves to hunt. The **Lemon Sole** is much lighter in colour.

Diet
Nocturnal feeders of invertebrates.

Thornback Ray
Raja clavata

Distribution
Eastern Atlantic, Mediterranean, Black Sea.

Habitat
Common in estuaries. Prefers sand and rocky bottoms. Can exceed depths of 300 feet.

Appearance
Kite shaped body with very vari-

Tub Gurnard
Trigia lucerna

Distribution
Eastern Atlantic, Mediterranean and Black Sea.

Tub gurnard

Tope/School Shark

Habitat
Favours inshore waters up to 500 feet. Prefers sandy or rocky bottoms

Appearance
Red body with striking blue pectoral fins. Large head with a pointed snout. Three spines on the lower fin look like crabs legs.

Diet
Invertebrates, also small fish.

Appearance
Light blue-green body fading to yellow and silver underside. Often a small dark spot at the upper base of the pectoral fin. Sometimes a small chin barbule.

Diet
Small invertebrates

Whiting
Merlangius merlangus

Distribution
North Atlantic, Black Sea, Aegean Sea, Adriatic Sea.

Habitat
Coastal waters up to depths of 200m. Prefers mud and gravel bottoms.

Whiting

On the Fly

On the Fly

Of all the ways there are to catch fish, fly fishing is the most graceful. Just about anyone who sees a fly fisherman wants to find out how to do it, but although it is easy enough to pick up the basics, fly fishing is no different to other branches of the sport in that it takes a lifetime to become an expert. The good news is that today, fly rods are available to suit every pocket and there are some very useful outfits out there that won't break the bank, so you can get started pretty cheaply. It wasn't always so, and even twenty years ago, a decent fly rod cost an arm and a leg, but now you can get a complete outfit for less than £100, although as with all these things, the sky is the limit and it is quite possible to pay seven timmuch for a rod alone; just don't forget that the only thing the fish gets to see is the fly...

The most confusing thing about fly fishing is the way the sport is divided into 'wet' and 'dry' fly fishing, but all this really means is that some flies are fished under the surface (wet), while others are fished on top (dry). Dry fly fishing used to be the almost exclusive preserve of southern English chalk stream fishermen, but since the war it has become a widely used technique and these days you can see it employed to catch everything from stocked reservoir trout in Essex to steelhead on the west coast of America. There isn't any magic to dry fly fishing, apart from the need to keep your fly afloat. In many respects it is easier than using a wet fly, although the dry fly purists wouldn't have you believe that.

Despite the fact that dry fly fishing is good fun and you can actually see the fish take, the vast majority of fish are caught on a wet fly – simply because fish spend most of their time feeding under the surface, rather than indulging in the chancy game of trying to catch insects that might fly off the surface any second. Wet fly fishing is a very diverse sport indeed, ranging from the use of traditional 'winged' wet flies on the Scottish lochs, through sight-fishing nymphs in clear water, to Atlantic salmon fly fishing – the vast majority of which uses a wet fly.

Don't believe that the only fish you can catch on a fly are salmon and trout. In the UK, many freshwater fish can be caught on a fly, including chub, perch, carp and barbel; while in the US, flies are one of the most popular methods used in the exciting sport of largemouth bass fishing. The explosion of interest in the sport has taken fly fishing far beyond fresh water in recent years and flies are used on a regular basis to catch saltwater species, including bonefish, permit and even tarpon. You can even catch marlin on a fly, although it is questionable whether the term is really appropriate for the massive lures that marlin fly fishermen use.

If you get into fly fishing, the fun doesn't stop at the waterside, because the winter months can be whiled away learning how to tie your own flies, another hobby which can be learnt quickly, but can prove so absorbing that some people give up fly fishing more or less completely and tie flies for competitions instead. The pinnacle of fly tying is to be able to tie what are known as 'fully-dressed' salmon flies, incredibly complex patterns, most of which date back to the 19th century, although new ones are being invented all the time. Some of these flies are an absolute riot of colour and few of them can be created with less than a dozen different materials to hand.

Some folk try to present fly fishing as somehow being better than coarse fishing, but the fact of the matter is that both methods are equally enjoyable and there is no reason for fly fishermen to look down on coarse fishermen, or vice versa. There aren't many people who have the talent to be good at both ways of fishing and the best compliment anyone can pay a fisherman, in my view, is to call them an 'all-rounder'. To be able to walk down to a water and catch fish in it, whatever method is needed, be it float, fly, or spinning, really does take some skill and there is as much fun to be had catching gudgeon on a maggot as there is hooking the biggest tarpon the ocean has to offer. Don't forget that the idea is to enjoy yourself!

Choosing a Fly Rod

There are several factors to consider when selecting a rod. It's important to choose one that is appropriate for both your fishing style and the fish you want to catch.

ACTION

This is the way in which a rod reacts when it is put under pressure during a cast or whilst bringing in a fish. A rod's flexibility is determined by its design and the material used. There are three main categories:

• A fast actioned fly rod will impart a high line speed to the fly line to cast long distances with tight loops. However, this type of rod can be quite stiff (potentially leading to more flies breaking off during casting) and requires good timing to avoid tangles. Not for beginners.

• A slow actioned fly rod will not cast as far, but is more forgiving and easier to cast with. It is also better for casting short distances as it will still flex with relatively little line out.

• A medium actioned fly rod gives the best of both worlds. Capable of good distances and tidy loops, it is suitable for most fishing styles.

MATERIAL

Most fly rods are now made from carbon fibre, which is stiffer than glass fibre, allowing for thinner, lighter designs with a faster action. Traditional split cane rods are now rare, not to mention expensive, and require a great deal of care.

FLY ROD LENGTH

It's possible to buy rods ranging from six to fifteen feet in length from most specialist outlets. Rods between eight feet and nine feet six inches with a slow-moderate action account for the majority of sales and are perfect for most fly fishers' needs. Rods less than eight feet long are ideal for fishing in narrow confines or in areas where there are overhanging trees. Longer lengths with a fast action in general give greater

AFTM Code	Weight (Grains) First 30 feet of your Flyline
1	60
2	80
3	100
4	120
5	140
6	160
7	185
8	210
9	240
10	280
11	330
12	380
13	440
14	500
15	550

range and are more suited to bigger rivers, bigger fish (such as salmon) and open waters.

A Good Rule of Thumb
River Fishing: up to 9 ft. Long casting isn't the objective here. Choose a lightweight rod that will make it easy to do lots of short distance casting.
Small Stillwater: 9 ft–9 ft 6. A good length of fly rod that will accurately cover feeding fish and cast reasonable distances. Suitable for most larger river and reservoir work.
Large Stillwater: 9 ft 6–10 ft. Good for heavier reservoir fishing, or salmon fishing.
Boat fishing: 10 ft or longer. The extra length in these fly rods helps keep the line in the air for cleaner casting.

LINE WEIGHT
Rods and lines are matched by the stiffness of the rod and the weight of the line. In general, rods designed for catching larger species are rated for heavier lines. The 'weight' is printed by the manufacturer on the rod. Lines come in numbered sizes from 1–16 based on the American Fishing Tackle Manufacturers' Association (AFTMA) industry standard. In essence, each AFTM number is a measure of the weight of the first thirty feet of fly line. Grains, still used in the US and Canada to measure gunpowder, are the unit of measurement used for line weights. The lower the line weight, the smaller the fly and the smaller the target should be; a higher line weight is needed for bigger fish.

A Good Rule of Thumb
1–3: Perfect for small dry flies and nymph fishing on gentle waters, but difficult to cast in any kind of wind.
4–6: Ideal for most trout fishing.
7–8: The extra power is suitable for catching grilse, or for bigger trout on reservoirs.
9–10: Enough strength to tackle salmon and pike.
11–16: For very big fish – double-handed salmon rods and single-handed saltwater rods.

Above: A close-up of fittings on a Hardy Angel TE 9 ft, 5 weight fly rod.

Below top: A Hardy Angel 8 ft, 3 weight trout fly rod. Perfect for trout less than half a pound or so, and also ideal for Parr.

Bottom: A Hardy Zane (after Zane Gray, author and passionate fisherman) 9 ft, 12 weight saltwater fly rod – for big fish like permit and tarpon.

Fly Fishing Reels

Below left: *A classic Hardy trout fly reel. Often criticized for not having an exposed rim (and only a basic click drag) this is more than adequate for loch and the vast majority of river and reservoir trout fishing. The label tells you what sort of line is on the reel – essential if you have a drawer full of trout reels.*

Below centre: *A more modern version of the same concept, this time with a disc drag. It costs more but doesn't guarantee you'll catch any more trout. Note that it has an exposed rim, so you can brake with the palm of your hand.*

Below right: *The full Monty. This is a two-weight Loop fly reel with a large arbour, exposed rim and sophisticated drag mechanism. Great fun for small trout dry fly fishing.*

Because the fly fisher casts with one hand whilst stripping the line from the reel with the other, the reel plays no part in the casting process and is sometimes considered a less important component of the fly fisherman's tackle box. Yet an ill-chosen reel can certainly lower your success rate.

Factors to consider when choosing a reel
• The weight of the reel (this must be matched to the weight of the rod and line, as any imbalance can affect the casting technique).
• How easy it is to change spools.
• A powerful drag mechanism isn't necessary for trout and most salmon fishing, although it is essential for saltwater fishing.
• Whatever species you intend to fish for, the drag should be smooth.

Most fly fishermen opt for a type of **centrepin reel**. Today's fly reels owe much to the pioneering narrow spooled design patented by the American Charles F. Orvis in 1874, and modified a year later to include a click mechanism to prevent the reel from overrunning. Despite technological advancements, the essential principle of the reel has remained the same over time – a rotating handle spins the spool which revolves around a single centre pin and in turn retrieves the line.

Usually the gear ratio is 1:1. The trout fisherman will find a simple single action fly reel with a limited adjustable drag is perfect as a means of storing the line, but bigger, more powerful fish pose a different problem.

Additional features on modern fly reels
• More sophisticated drag systems, increasing the range of adjustment.
• The use of lighter, high performance composite materials like aluminium and graphite.
• Large arbor spools to reduce the effects of line memory and make it easier and quicker to retrieve a powerful catch.

OTHER TYPES OF FLY REEL
Geared fly reels Manufactured with a higher gear ratio to allow for faster retrieval of the catch.
Automatic fly reels With the simple flick of the lever, the line is retrieved automatically. Weighty and not popular with many fishermen as they aren't good for playing anything except relatively small fish.

A very high-end trout fly reel by Ari 't Hart. At the cutting edge of reel design and technology these are exclusive and expensive

Fly Fishing Lines

Fluorescent lines spooled onto a pair of modern reels.

Early lines were made of horsehair or braided silk threads. In 1939, nylon monofilament lines were developed, and this remains the material of choice today – though that doesn't mean that buying a line is a straight-forward business. Flick through any tackle catalogue and you will find a dozen types of floaters, a breathtaking range of sinkers, 'intermediates', 'wind cutters', 'nymph tips', Spey lines, 'triangle tapers' and even lines designed for individual species of fish. Most will be available in double taper and weight forward versions, but you'll also see finishes, and lengths that vary from twenty-seven to over forty-five yards. The termi-nology can be bewildering, but a line has just six essential properties:

Weight Lines are matched to rods by weight using the AFTMA system (see page 83). You won't go far wrong by trusting the manufacturer's rating, though there is an argument that going up a line weight often loads the rod better and can have a beneficial impact on your casting.

Length Trout lines have standardized at around thirty yards. Longer lines can overflow the reel and need to be cut down to size before use; shorter ones give more space for backing. Salmon lines are longer – thirty-five to forty yards is more than enough for the average caster, although much longer lines are available for Spey casting. Lines with interchangeable tip sections allow rapid alterations of tactics to match the conditions.

Colour Theory suggests that the lighter the line the lower the visibility, but it is arguably more important to choose a line that you can see than one that the fish can't. In truth, there's little evidence to suggest that the colour of your line makes any difference to your chances of success, but a dull, matt finish is thought to be more effective.

Taper Line taper allows a smooth transfer of energy from the rod to the fly. A perfectly parallel line will transform even the most competent caster into a bungling idiot. There are several taper profiles. The 'double taper' tapers at both ends with a level section in the middle. It is the easiest of all to cast and mend, but it is not ideal for distance casting and the thick middle section can make it challenging to handle in a wind. The 'shooting head' has a short taper at the front of the line. It is highly specialized and best used by skilled casters looking to reach long distances, usually with a double-haul cast. The 'weight forward' is the most common variety, and combines the finesse of the double taper and the distance casting properties of the shooting head – and is less likely to tangle. Within this format you'll find more sophisticated variants named after fish species, as well as 'nymph' and 'bug' lines. Under most conditions, you can't beat a conservatively tapered weight forward.

Density The basic distinction here is between 'intermediates' and 'sinkers'. There is no firm definition of what qualities an intermediate line should have, but in essence it is a line that just sinks. Conventional sinkers tend to sink unevenly – the body faster than the tip – and 'density' or 'weight compensated' lines, where the whole line is designed to sink uniformly, have been put forward as a solution. Uneven sink rates are less of an issue for river, reservoir and deep lake anglers, but if you do a lot of nymphing on still water, a density compensated sinking line might prove to be a good investment. Most manufacturers also market a range of 'sink tip' lines, combining a sinking tip section with a floating belly. However, the fact that the majority of the line floats limits how far the tip can sink, and they can be tricky to cast. Similar results can be achieved with a long sinking leader and a weighted fly – at a considerable saving.

Suppleness The ideal line should have no 'memory' – it should not spring off the reel in coils – and it should lie limp in the hand, with no tendency to twist. Twenty years ago, such a line would have been fought over in a tackle shop, but advances in material mean most modern fly lines comply. Be careful buying 'mill end' lines, as all too often these are made using outmoded technology and have inherited all the ills of their grandfathers.

LEADER

This is the shorter section tied between the end of the line and the fly, bait or lure. Depending on the material used they can serve two purposes. An additional length of monofilament ensures the cast is as delicate as possible, while a wire leader gives extra strength and resistance, useful when fighting fish with ferocious teeth, sharp scales or scything tails.

A Hardy saltwater fly line in and out of its box. This example is a twelve weight – perfect for bigger fish like tarpon and permit.

Selecting a Fly

I doubt there is a fly fisher in the land whose pockets aren't bulging with fly boxes stuffed with dozens of patterns that will never be knotted onto the end of a leader, let alone find their way into the mouth of a fish. This isn't an accident – most of the patterns out there are designed to catch fishermen, not fish, and they work. All of us buy more flies than we need, but the problem beginners face is choosing a working selection from the thousands of patterns on offer. The truth is that you can be a successful fly fisher with a very small selection of different flies, because the way you fish them is almost as important as the fly you are fishing; to quote the famous John Selwyn Marryat, 'It is not the fly, it's the driver!'

You will, of course, need different selections for different fish and depending on which species you are after, you may well need both dry and wet flies in your box. The key message here is that fish aren't entomologists and they are very likely to sample anything that looks about right and is fished at the right level, so on most occasions it isn't essential to have an exact imitation of a particular insect attached to the end of your line. Fish are opportunists and, in the competitive world they live in, they can't look gift horses in the mouth too often.

The main reason why some anglers catch more trout than others is not because they are fishing the 'right' flies, but because they are fishing the right way and know how to spot a take, because many takes are so subtle that you won't feel a thing – but strike when you see a slight flattening of the water and, as if by magic, a fish is on.

Changing flies at the side of an Irish lough whilst fishing for brown trout. Perhaps it will bring a change of fortune?

It is a different story for salmon fishing, where the size of the fly is usually more important than the pattern, although the depth you fish at is also critical. But salmon hook themselves and, unlike trout, it is quite possible to catch them by feel alone. They pull – you pull back!

The step beyond is learning to tie your own flies. Most fly fishermen don't do this, either because they think it is too difficult, or because they think they don't have enough time, but it is a relaxing pastime on a winter evening with a whisky to hand and there is nothing more satisfying than catching a fish on a fly you tied the night before.

A tackle box filled with flies and ready to go.

Tying Your Own Fly

Above: *A fly tying vice, complete with a dry fly in the process of being tied.*

Opposite: *A brown trout launches an attack on a fly whilst the angler looks on.*

Two hundred years ago, everybody tied their own flies, because there was no alternative: if you wanted to catch trout, you either had to learn how to wrap a feather around a hook, or stick to worming. Even if you did know how to tie flies, getting the materials wasn't easy and fishermen spent as much time skulking around farmyards eyeing up roosters as they did wetting their lines. Vices were rarely used and most anglers held the hook pinched between the finger and thumb of one hand while they wrapped materials around it with the other, hoping all the while that their womenfolk didn't notice that their sewing boxes had emptied of silk and the cat was going bald. The lack of choice of materials meant that there were fewer patterns available and fishermen used a much narrower selection than we do now, but they caught just as many fish, because trout and salmon don't care as much about patterns as fly fishermen do.

Nowadays, there's no need to kidnap fowl and pull out their neck feathers, because commercial enterprises like Whiting Farms offer the most fantastic selection of 'genetic' capes, tying thread is available in just about any colour, and man-made materials are revolutionizing the market. If you want something, you only have to pick up the phone. Where once there was hardly any choice, there is now too much, and the main problem most beginners have is deciding what pattern to use. In many ways, fishermen were better off back in the 18th century, when the fly they fished with was the one they had.

Learning to tie your own flies isn't difficult, just as long as you remember that we are sterner critics of our productions than the fish. It doesn't cost a fortune to take tying lessons, and a few questions at the local fishing club should get you connected. You can spend a fortune buying materials, especially if you turn into a hackle junkie, but a few quid is enough to get started. And although I don't have the patience for it myself, there must be something very satisfying about taking your own designs out and catching fish with them when no-one else has had a bite.

the rod. Alternatively, the thumb may be placed directly on top of the rod. This variation is particularly useful when additional downward pressure is needed to propel the line forward.

BASIC CASTS

There are two basic fly fishing casts which should be understood and practised until they become automatic:

Straight line (or overhead) cast This involves two movements – a straight line back cast followed by a forward cast with a pause in between. For a successful cast, the angler must follow the same straight path, beginning with the rod at around 09.00 (on a clock face) or slightly lower. Rod, hand, wrist and lower arm move in unison, accelerating vertically in an arc pivoting around the elbow and shoulder to around 11.30. Here the wrist 'breaks' sharply, with the speed of the rod tip increasing markedly, driving the rod back to 12.30. The line should now be flying upwards, backwards and will extend absolutely straight in mid-air. During the forward cast the wrist remains in the 'broken' position and accelerates again once it reaches the 11.00 mark. The 'stop' should be made crisply at 10.00, allowing the line to extend straight with a well-formed loop uncoiling directly above the line from the rod tip.

Roll cast A circular motion cast that changes the direction of the line. Instead of a straight line, the roll cast demands a tensioned curved loop, known as a 'D' loop. The 'D' loop is anchored by water contact, allowing the power stroke to deliver sufficient energy to unroll the line. The rod mustn't 'stop' or the tension will be lost and the cast will fail. Instead the rod changes direction and speed, turning as the cast is made to form the loop. There should be no slack in the loop when the forward cast is made.

Simple roll casts of a short distance can be made with a stationary loop of line drooping to the water surface from the rod tip. This is also a good method of straightening the line in preparation for a longer cast. Longer roll casts are made by forming the loop and delivering the power stroke in one continuous upward motion to ensure that the line is propelled clear of the water.

A well executed roll cast should send the line high, straight and true, away from the angler, similar to the overhead cast. Because the cast does not require much space it is ideal for fishing in restricted spaces.

OTHER CASTS

Spey cast Beyond the fact that it was developed on Scotland's River Spey, the exact origins of the Spey cast are a little cloudy. It has certainly evolved through the years and has become much more widely practised with the advent of lighter graphite and carbon rods. Spey casting is the most commonly used 'change of direction roll casting' technique. Both single and double Spey casts depend on the principle that the 'D' loop direction is changed to approximate the direction of the forward cast, which is then completed like any other roll cast.

Single Spey cast The single Spey cast achieves the change of angle by moving the line from the 'fished out' position downstream of the angler, by a semi-circular sweeping movement to place the 'D' loop on the upstream side, with the anchor point further upstream than the intended delivery angle. Thus it avoids any possibility of the line that is being cast crossing the line that is in contact with the water. Otherwise a tangle is very likely to result. Perfecting the 'D' loop with the anchor point in the correct location is the secret of good Spey casting but also the most difficult part to learn.

Most beginners put too much effort into the process of making the 'D' loop, it is really quite a gentle action, almost 'floating' the line through the air into the correct position with a controlled underhand loop. Too much speed or power and the loop will not form properly and most likely it will not anchor in the correct place. Use the roll casting loading method to form the loop, swing out and upstream. As you do so the tip of the rod will naturally dip to cause the line to alight and anchor, when the line touches down, raise the rod to complete the 'D' loop and keep it airborne, keep your rhythm and deliver the forward stroke tangentially to the top of the 'D' loop. Practise with small changes of direction to begin with. Gradually increase the change of direction as timing and technique improves. For any set of circumstances, there is a maximum size of 'D' loop that can be created. Often the angler will want to cast further than that amount and so the line must be shot to achieve long casts.

Because the loop is formed upstream, it is suitable and safe for an upstream wind and for a gentle or non-threatening downstream wind, providing that the angler is capable of controlling the 'D' loop to keep the fly well away from his person and safe during the cast. In a strong wind this becomes impossible and the Single Spey cast is very dangerous.

Double Spey cast Cope with downstream winds by using the double Spey cast. The stronger the wind, the easier this cast becomes, but it is best not used with an upstream wind at all. For a Double Spey cast the 'D' loop is positioned at the downstream side of the angler by first moving the rod upstream almost parallel to the water surface to create enough slack to form the 'D' loop when the rod is swung downstream again. The rod is then swept downstream, round the downstream side of the angler forming the 'D' loop in the process before assuming the roll casting position and completing the cast. As the line is reversed round the angler and raised to form the loop the angler watches the ripple that is caused by the line tearing from the water downstream. When the ripple stops, the maximum amount of line is airborne and the anchor point contact is minimum. This is the time to turn the rod into the forward cast and complete the roll.

Underhand cast Invented by Swede Goran Andersson, the Underhand cast also uses the 'D loop' principle. It is in the method of loading the rod that the Underhand cast differs by its use of shooting heads joined by loops to the fly line. The principle is to use an appropriate length of shooting head to form the 'D loop', during which time the comparatively short head is entirely suspended between the rod tip and the surface of the water, the necessary "anchor" being provided by the fly and leader alone. Because the "anchor" is minimised the line lifts very easily. In order to achieve a high line speed over a comparatively short forward stroke a fairly fast actioned rod is best.

In traditional Spey and Roll casting the energy is delivered to the rod by both hands; during the underhand cast most of the movement is produced by the lower (or under hand) in the case of the double handed casts, and by forward hauling during the single handed casts.

Light and efficient to use, the main disadvantage of the underhand cast lies in the retrieval and management of the shooting line.

Top: *The late Hugh Falkus begins a single Spey cast by drawing the line back towards him having fished out the previous cast.*

Middle: *The rod is loading now as Hugh begins the process of forming the loop.*

Bottom: *The loop is now formed, ready for the forward cast. The rod is quite far back, but Hugh, being a very experienced caster, won't run into problems because of it.*

Top: *Hugh begins the roll part of the Spey cast by punching the rod forwards and dropping his hands down about a foot to form the casting loop.*

Middle: *The line shoots out as the loaded rod catapults it off the water.*

Bottom: *A second after this shot was taken, the line was on the water.*

Salmon Fishing in Scotand

The author of the *Treatyse of Fysshynge with an Angle*, published in 1496, described the salmon as 'a noble fish, but difficult to catch'. Given that Dame Juliana Berners, who is reputed to have written this, the very first book on fishing to be printed in English, was a nun and fished with horsehair lines tied to the end of a six-foot hazel wand, we can take her at her word. In those far-off days, long before the reel was invented, if you hooked a salmon, the only alternative to hanging on was to throw your rod in the water and chase it downstream until the fish either exhausted itself or threw the hook.

Nowadays, we have much better gear and have the chance to fight salmon on equal terms, but that doesn't alter the most peculiar fact about salmon fishing, which is that they don't eat at all in fresh water. No-one has the faintest clue why salmon take a fly, or what they take it for, although all sorts of theories have been advanced, ranging from Arthur Ransome's idea that they took them for elvers, to the more modern view that the sight of a fly or lure arouses some basic instinct in the fish which prompts them to take. It is certainly the case that if you cast often enough at a particular fish, it can sometimes be induced to strike, even if it has been in its lie for many days.

Of course, you don't have to fish for salmon with a fly – more than half of all these fish caught in the UK are probably caught on a spinner and worming for salmon is a speciality of its own, although it is frowned upon in certain circles and it is probably better not to turn up on the smarter beats armed with a worming rod.

Whichever way you choose to catch them, salmon are very special fish. They spawn in fresh water, yet live in the salt (curiously, eels do exactly the opposite, but that is another story); they travel thousands of miles, can dive as deep as any nuclear submarine and can jump half a dozen feet in the air, a feat which few submarines can match. They navigate by the stars and by magnetism and by methods we don't yet understand and then, when they are within range of the outflow of their parent river, they literally smell their way home. So give them respect, there are few creatures like them.

The Life-Cycle of the Scottish Salmon

Young salmon, known as fry, spawned in the upper reaches of Scottish rivers are hatched amongst the gravel beds until, as parr, they move into deeper pools. After two or three years, now known as smolts and ranging from 100 to 150mm in length, they swim down river in April and May. Once they reach the open sea they migrate northwards and then westwards for many thousands of miles. These epic journeys can take one and sometimes two years and some tagged fish from Scottish rivers have been recorded as far as the Canadian Arctic between the Western coast of Greenland and Baffin Island. They feed and grow in these cold northern oceans and between one and three years later their homing instinct is switched on and they make the return journey across the Atlantic to the river where they were spawned, spawning themselves in late autumn or early winter in the same area where they lived as parr. The female turns on her side and fans the gravel and small stones of the stream bed, creating a depression to make a nest. Cock salmon, who have been shadowing the female as she returns to the spawning grounds fertilize the eggs as they are shed. The female

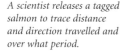

A scientist releases a tagged salmon to trace distance and direction travelled and over what period.

then covers the nest with gravel and the cycle starts once more.

What is unique to the Scottish salmon is the length of the season. Most salmon re-enter their home rivers in the summer and early autumn, but in Scotland they do so throughout the year. It is possible to fish for salmon in every month of the year with the exception of December, when no fishing is allowed to protect the spawning fish. The rivers of the east coast of Scotland are home to the greater number of the world's spring or early-running salmon.

Above: *A school of migrating smolts. After several years, and having reached a size of about four inches, the parrs become smolts and begin migrating downriver to the sea.*

Following pages: *A group of Atlantic salmon swims upstream to spawn.*

This page, clockwise from below: *Salmon in a trawl net – a hazard on the way back to the spawning grounds; a salmon leaping over a weir on its way upriver; once at the spawning grounds a female Atlantic salmon turns on its side to dislodge sand and gravel to make a nest, or redd, for its eggs.*

Opposite above: *a detail of the distinctive hooked lip of a male Atlantic salmon in the breeding cycle.*

Opposite below: *male and female salmon (foreground) releasing their milt and eggs over the nest.*

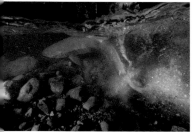

The River Tay

Some of the world's finest Atlantic salmon fishing is to be found in the sixth-longest river in Britain, which winds for 117 miles from Loch Tay through the Scottish Highlands and Perthshire countryside to its mouth in the Firth of Tay. In 1922, Georgina Ballantine caught a 64-pound fish on the Glendelvine beat – which remains the British record for a rod-caught salmon. A 27.5-pound salmon was caught on Loch Tay on the opening day of the season in 2000. At 7,000 cubic feet a second, it has the greatest flow of any river in the country. It is one of the most prolific salmon rivers; the nets, which used to catch such huge numbers of fish – 90,000 were netted from the river in 1969 – have been gone since 1997.

Big runs of fresh fish enter the Tay and also the River Earn in the late summer and autumn. Most are grilse of around six to ten pounds or salmon of about 15–20 pounds, with the prospect of fish up to 30 pounds. The biggest catches of the season are taken then, especially in the lower Tay. Like in many of the famous Scottish salmon rivers, brown trout and sea trout fishing is also excellent, with the latter often being caught up to ten pounds. For information on the various salmon beats along the Tay and its various tributaries, including detailed catch statistics, see http://www.fishtay.co.uk/

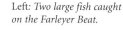

Left: *Two large fish caught on the Farleyer Beat.*

Above: *Fishing the Taymount Beat in the morning mist above Campsie Lin. I have been fishing this beat for the last fifteen years.*

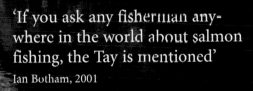

'If you ask any fisherman any-where in the world about salmon fishing, the Tay is mentioned'

Ian Botham, 2001

Ian Botham opens the Tay fishing season in 2001 with the traditional quaich of whisky.

Since the 1860s the start of the Scottish Salmon Fishing season has been marked on 15th January by a symbolic ceremony in the tiny village of Kenmore. Locals and anglers brave the icy conditions and head for the shore of Loch Tay, where the salmon and the river are toasted with a quaich of whisky. In 2001 I performed the traditional blessing to start the season. Although the ceremony was put back in 2007 due to unseasonably mild water temperatures which disrupted spawning patterns, it returned to 15th January in 2008.

The River Tweed

Fly fishing on the Tweed with Sir Walter Scott's Abbotsford in the background. Sir Walter had come to Abbotsford in 1811 and shortly afterwards he wrote: 'I happened to want some fishing-tackle for the use of a guest, when it occurred to me to search the old writing-desk already mentioned, in which I used to keep articles of that nature. I got access to it with some difficulty; and in looking for lines and flies, the long-lost manuscript presented itself. I immediately set to work to complete it, according to my original purpose.' The bestselling Waverley *was published in 1814.*

Although it actually flows through England for twenty-three of its ninety-seven miles (nineteen of those along the south bank only), the Tweed is considered the second longest river in Scotland. It has the distinction of producing more fish caught to the fly than any other river in the UK. The salmon catch is nothing short of phenomenal, an annual average of 14,500 recorded fish in the last five years and a high in 2007 of over 16,000 – the highest recorded figure since 1952 and a record for any British river. The high numbers are attributed to a range of conservation initiatives and a catch and return policy that saw 9,000 fish being returned last year. But the high numbers also reflected a high proportion of late summer and autumn grilse, smaller fish returning to the river after their first winter at sea, and fewer large fish that have spent several years at sea. The upper Tweed and Etterick had reduced catches, the middle beats were stable and the lower Tweed saw a better than average year. The Junction beat on the lower Tweed, including the Hempseedford beat, provide a mile and a half of excellent boat and double bank fishing. The catches on Junction are remarkable, with a five-year average of some 835 salmon and grilse and fifty-four sea trout. The Junction Pool itself, arguably the most famous salmon pool in the world, can hold an enormous number of fish given the right water conditions.

Brown trout, both stocked and wild, are mostly in the three-quarters to one pound range, but can be caught up to five pounds. Sea trout start running in June/July and by the autumn can reach twelve pounds or more.

For information on the various salmon beats along the Tweed and its various tributaries, including detailed catch statistics, see http://www.fishtweed.co.uk/

Tweed valley, Elibank, the traditional home of the hideous 'Muckle-Moothed Meg' after whom the drab 'Meg with the Muckle Mooth' salmon fly is named.

The River Dee

Rising in the Cairngorms at a spring at the Wells of Dee and flowing through 'Royal Deeside', so-called because of the Royal residence at Balmoral, this Aberdeenshire river is eighty-seven miles long. It has a succession of varied pools, some rocky and some gravelly, interspersed by sharp rapids; all forming ideal water for fly fishing. Its waters are, except when in spate, crystal-clear and for some reason do not become peat-stained like that of its larger neighbour, the Spey, Since the 17th century anglers have been enjoying its famous salmon run as well as excellent summer fishing for salmon, grilse and sea trout. It is the home of greased line salmon fishing, developed at Cairnton by Arthur Wood, who pioneered the revolutionary technique of floating lines and floating

Below: Craithie Beat, the old Brig' O' Dee at Invercauld.

flies in the years before the First World War. High numbers of salmon are caught compared with many Scottish rivers, the summer salmon and grilse being the most abundant. As in many Scottish rivers, the numbers of late summer grilse have been increasing. The runs of sea trout start arriving in May. There is some coarse fishing on Aboyne Loch, where pike weighing over thirty pounds are caught each year. The river is rocky and wading can be difficult – a wading staff and lifejacket are recommended.

For information on the various salmon beats along the Dee and its various tributaries, including detailed catch statistics, see http://www.fishdee.co.uk/

Below: *The new Princess Diana receives a lesson in fly fishing from the head ghillie at Balmoral in 1981.*
Below Left: *Queen Elizabeth the Queen Mother happy doing what she liked to do.*

Royal Deeside

The royal family have been regular summer visitors to Balmoral and the waters of the Dee. The late Queen Mother learnt to fish as a child, was a passionate fisher-woman and would always make time on her overseas trips to take in some local fishing. A particular favourite were her three visits to New Zealand. During her last visit in 1966 she was famously photographed on Lake Wanaka fishing whilst wearing pearls.

The River Dee was where the press began to believe that the romance between Lady Diana Spencer and the

Prince of Wales had become a serious matter. Invited to Balmoral for a long weekend in September 1980, she joined Charles on the river for some fly fishing on Sunday 7th September. A photographer spotted them fishing together and on the Monday the couple's romance hit the headlines.

The River Spey

Above: Playing a fish on the Spey – and finally netting it: an autumn salmon.

Opposite: Fishing the Spey at sunrise as the morning mist disperses.

Snow-fed from the Cairngorms, the Spey rises to the west of Laggan in the Monadhliath mountains and is the fastest flowing river in Scotland. A classic salmon river with some 8,000 fish taken each year, the river lends its name to a particular technique of casting (a type of change of direction roll casting usually where there is no room for a back or overhead cast) which was developed on the river in the 19th century and is still widely practised today. The ability to Spey cast is particularly useful on tree-lined pools. The Spey becomes a big river in its lower reaches where a 13–15 foot double handed fly rod is the most commonly used. It has an unusually fast stream, and from the mid point to the sea it is the fastest of any British river. Its tributaries, particularly its main tributary the Avon, which attracts a good run of salmon and sea trout from April onwards, and Dulnain, are excellent salmon rivers in their own right. The Spey, like most Scottish salmon rivers, can be expensive, but there is also some of the best, and reasonably priced, Association water available in Scotland. And, like the other salmon rivers, it is suffering from faltering spring runs. As a result in many areas fish caught before the first of June are subject to new conservation measures and must be returned. However, September to the end of the season will see fish run the rivers every day.

For information on the various salmon beats along the Spey and its various tributaries, including detailed catch statistics, see http://www.fishspey.co.uk/ and http://www.speycaster.net/

Trout Fishing in British Rivers

Everyone has fished for them at one time or another – feisty little firm-fleshed trout that run three or four to the pound and fight like fish twice their weight. They are the sharks of the small streams, the tuna of the lochs; and like their bigger cousins, they neither give nor take any quarter. Whichever way you look at it, they are among the most sporting creatures it is possible to catch with a rod and line, and they bore deep and leap high, driven by a spirit few other fish can match.

In the small streams of the dales and the high moorland, a half-pound trout may well be several years old and be the largest predator his particular ecosystem can support. To become the terror of his pool, our half-pounder will have accumulated a lifetime's experience of living on his wits and, though small, he won't be easy to catch. Sure, there are days when one can fish a loch and take any number of fish like him, but bags like that are uncommon, and dour days are more often accounted for by small brownies' survival skills than anything else.

Yet, on the other hand, a whole generation of anglers has grown up fishing for stocked rainbows with eight weight rods and has become conditioned to the idea that a trout isn't a trout unless it runs into double figures, though there is some serious fun to be had catching smaller fish using light tackle. The same reservoirs usually hold good stocks of one or two pound fish, again, usually rainbows, but with a mixture of browns in the more enlightened fisheries. These smaller trout rarely make it into the angling reports, but they are the bread and butter of trout fishing as I know it and in many places they offer more fun than their larger cousins, because they often rise freely and, if the water is clear enough, can be taken with the most exciting method of all – sight fishing with a nymph on light tackle.

Although most of the trout fishing in the UK is for stocked rainbows, brown trout are one of our most successful exports and, thanks to ambitious programmes completed over a century ago, they can be found all over the world, as far afield as New Zealand and North America – so a trout rod in your bag is a ticket to pure enjoyment.

Chalk Streams

Chalk Streams

A chalk stream is a specific type of watercourse found only in the British Isles, France and New Zealand. In England they flow largely from the chalk hills of southern and eastern England where they are typified by braided channels, many the relics of historic water meadows. Water soaks through the porous subsurface chalk and is stored in aquifers which feed the source of each river. Its particular ecological characteristics include a consistent temperature and flow. Generally the water, though mineral-rich, is free of sandy deposits and strikingly clear. The alkaline water is extremely fertile and home to lots of water plants and a plentiful insect population, conditions that are perfect for

Left: *Fishing the River Test, with great concentration, at King's Somborne, Hampshire.*

Below: *A manicured bank beside the still waters of the River Test.*

fly fishing, in particular dry fly fishing. Over time these streams have been carefully managed to sustain large numbers of wild brown trout and grayling as well as stocked brown and rainbow trout. Many of these rivers once had salmon as well as trout, but there have been great changes to agricultural practices. For example, in 1988 over four thousand fish ran the Frome. By 2004, that had fallen to seven hundred and fifty. The increase in acreage devoted to maize and winter cereals leaves the soil exposed to heavy winter rains, which washes silt into the rivers' gravel beds and suffocates the fish eggs.

The season of fishing for trout on the chalk streams usually begins in late April and lasts until the end of September, mostly using upstream dry flies and small nymphs. Almost all the fishing is in private hands, but day rods can be acquired on many beats either from the UK websites that specialize in offering chalk stream fishing or through tackle shops or hotels in the main centres.

A fisherman's bridge over a weir. The still and inviting waters of the mill pond are above the weir.

SOME TOP CHALK STREAM RIVERS

The Test, Hampshire

The main river itself flows for just under forty miles but with tributaries and backwaters slightly over double that. It is probably the most famous trout river in the world, famous for its prolific mayfly hatches (as described in *A Summer on the Test* by John Hills, published in 1921 and perhaps the best book on chalk stream fishing ever written). A group of anglers, chronicled by Frederick Halford in the 1880s and 90s, developed the sport of upstream fly fishing so it became, at the time, a rigid system and a method of fishing that spread around the world. Most fishing today is for large stocked brown trout and rainbows of two to six pounds, or more.

The Itchen, Hampshire

Flowing through some of England's most beautiful countryside, the Itchen is shorter than the Test but is also regarded as one of the finest chalk streams in the world. It is where the first artificial nymphs were developed by G. E. M. Skues in the late 19th century. Its pristine waters, which are used for growing watercress, are home to a range of protected species including the white-clawed crayfish and the brook Lamprey. Its mayflies hatch slightly earlier than those on the Test, although these hatches are a fraction of what they used to be.

The Kennet, Berkshire

The Kennet is a tributary of the Thames and famous for its large resident wild brown trout – fish of five pounds or more are taken each season. It provides very good fishing early in the season and again in September, as well as the end of the day in mid-summer. A hot summer's day requires the skill to fish with a weighted nymph.

The Frome, Dorset

This river's thirty-five miles of high quality waters support world-famous brown trout fishing, and at one time it held the British sea trout record. Much of the river requires wading to have room to cast, but recently a lot of work has been done to improve access and bank clearance.

Casting a fly on the river test at King's Somborne in Hampshire.

Fly Fishing Spate Rivers

The majority of free-flowing cold water courses in the world are classed as spate or freestone rivers. The name derives from the manner in which smooth stones, gravel and other debris from the river bed make up part of the flow. In the UK, the best spate rivers for trout fishing are to be found in western Wales, the far north of England and the east and west coasts of Scotland. Some sustain great supplies of wild brown trout and some also provide sea trout – known locally as sewin, peel or finnock. Typically the season runs from March to October. Tactics for resident browns are downstream wet fly and upstream nymph and dry fly. Small flies and larger lures fished on the surface or under, mostly from dusk onward, will take the sea-goers.

SOME TOP BRITISH SPATE RIVERS

The Don, Aberdeenshire, Scotland

Regarded as the best resident brown trout river in the UK and is also good for salmon and sea trout. Brown trout of up to three pounds are often caught, and much bigger fish from time to time. April and May are the best time for larger specimens, with early and late in the day in mid-summer also proving fruitful. There is a hatchery at Mill of Newe where native salmon, sea trout and brown trout are reared.

The Teifi, Wales

A river over seventy miles long which runs through some beautiful countryside, the Teifi is a mecca for sea trout (known locally as 'sewin') anglers, particularly at night as sea trout feed more readily under cover of darkness. In this straight, fast-flowing river, a pair of breathable chest waders, wading boots, a buoyancy aid and a torch are indispensable. The sea trout spawn from November onwards but may return to the spawning grounds as early as March, with the main run from May to July. Clear water recently subsided from spate together with a cloudy sky and muggy conditions are ideal. Extreme alertness is very important – the take

A summer grilse caught on the Lower Tindal beat, River Till.

SALMON

The biggest Atlantic salmon run in the early months of the year and weigh on average about nine pounds. They can be caught from January onwards in rivers such as the Drowes, which flows into Donegal Bay. As other rivers open, spring fish may be sought all over Ireland. They can also be caught in some loughs, and Lough Beltra, near Newport in County Mayo, can produce fine fish from March onwards.

Grilse are salmon which have spent one winter at sea and are a sporting game fish – swift, acrobatic and ready takers of a well presented fly. They weigh from about three pounds upwards, and are widely distributed. The timing of the main runs varies between river systems but most begin in June; this is when a fishery like Delphi in County Mayo can provide spectacular sport in a glorious setting. Irish grilse runs are some of the heaviest in western Europe and they offer the salmon fisherman his best chance of sport.

Generally salmon in river or lough take best when fresh in from the sea, but they can also be active after floods. Salmon may be caught on bait, spinner or fly, although some fisheries restrict anglers to fly only, except in certain water conditions. Bait is often used for early spring fish as rivers may then be high and coloured. The bait used may be natural or artificial depending on local regulations, and can be fished on a twelve or fifteen pound test line and a ten or eleven foot spinning rod. Similar tackle can be used for bait fishing throughout the season, but with lighter lines for grilse fishing in low water.

The services of a ghillie or guide are essential for the salmon angler on the loughs. Salmon will often be concentrated in known lies like the Black Rock on Lough Furnace at the Burrishoole fishery in County Mayo – they will rarely be evenly dispersed throughout a lough. The angler fishing these lies, who will usually be fly fishing, will need to have the boat's direction closely controlled; it cannot be left to drift before the wind. The angler will also need the boatman's help when a fish is hooked, as the boat must be rowed quickly to deeper water where the fish can be played out. A ten-foot (AFTM 7/8) or slightly longer single handed rod such as would be used for grilse fishing, matched with an intermediate or sink-tip line, will serve well for lough fishing.

Salmon have preferred lies in rivers, so the visiting salmon angler should seek the help of a guide for at least the first part of a trip.

To catch a spring salmon on the fly is one of the great experiences in angling. Usually fifteen-foot rods and number ten or eleven sinking lines will be required in early spring for Irish rivers such as the Blackwater in County Cork or the Laune in County Kerry, although shorter rods and lighter lines may be used on some rivers. Floating lines become necessary from late April when the water is warmer. Fly fishing for grilse will require either a double handed rod, or a ten-foot single handed rod carrying a number seven or eight floating or intermediate line. Leaders should be at least ten pounds test. A range of flies has been developed for Irish salmon fishing. The shrimp fly is a unique one used on many Irish rivers, notably the Moy in County Mayo, in varying patterns throughout the season; sizes vary from number six or eight flies in late spring to fourteen or sixteen flies in summer. The salmon and sea trout season opens on 1st January in some fisheries, but most open later (on various dates up to the 20th March). Most close on 30th September with some exceptions which close on various dates between 15th September and 12th October.

For further information, the Irish Fisheries Board provides a comprehensive and evocative, indeed model website for the whole of Ireland at http://www.cfb.ie/fishing_in_ireland/

Above: *Fishing an upland stream for brown trout in Connemara, County Galway. I have fished the Delphi System in Connemara on many occasions.*

Following pages: *A magnificent brownie. The fly box has a year's worth of permutations. The size of the fish means it was caught in one of the eastern rivers or the excellent loughs of the area, known collectively as 'The Great Western Lakes'.*

waters flowing in the rivers below. We landed by the riverbeds where possible and in some cases there was only enough room to hover over a rock while we hopped out. Once the helicopter left we were alone with only the sounds of the river and the occasional bird. The guides each carried a machete, which they used to break through the thick vegetation in places as we made our way upstream. The network of rivers provided pool after pool of crystal-clear water. In some cases the water was barely five feet wide, but held the most beautiful, and powerful, wild browns and rainbows. The guides would normally spot a fish with the help of polarized lenses, and then we would cast to them.

The fishing varied greatly in style, with different techniques required, though the common denominator was the clarity of the water. We were fishing both wet and dry flies, and sometimes we combined a dry fly over a nymph. Often the trout would just nudge the nymph and the take was missed in a fraction of a second, so we fabricated some bite indicators with some wool on the line. On many occasions we would watch a trout move from its lie and take the nymph or dry fly. At other times they were just uninterested. That's the beauty of fishing! Once hooked, however, in many cases for the first time in their lives, the wild trout fought long and hard. Sometimes we were only able to take one fish from a pool, and in other cases we could walk our way up, coaxing two or three out of the same pool before moving on.

At this time of year the temperature of the air and water is such that you can fish in a T-shirt and shorts or lightweight trousers, and wet-shoes which dried quickly in the warm sun. We would normally sit by the river and have a sandwich for lunch surrounded by the peace and tranquillity of the river. We walked four miles on average each day, often ascending quite rapidly, covering the pools and fish holding areas as we moved on. Every trout was returned to the water.

In the evening the helicopter pilot flew upstream to the morning drop-off point, or until he spotted the orange panel that the guide pulled out of his rucksack. It was such virgin territory on more than one occasion thick undergrowth and small trees had to be chopped back in order for the helicopter to be able to land. Then a flight back to the lodge, and a chance to reflect on another fabulous day's trout fishing in New Zealand – there really is no other place like it on earth.

Yet another massive rainbow trout, probably seven or eight pounds (though look at its girth – it is in beautiful condition), before being returned. On our worst day we caught six fish; on our best, over twenty.

Fly Fishing in the United States and Canada

Above: *Hat Creek, Northern California, a typical view of a wild rainbow trout water.*

Below: *Fishing the McCloud river in Northern California. A fifty-mile-long tributary of the Sacramento, it runs green because of glacier melt from the Cascade Mountains. The water temperature can be one degree off freezing when the air temperature is 100 degrees Fahrenheit.*

Fishing experience will vary enormously across such a vast continent. In the US there is a wealth of choice, from Alaska in the far north where there are strong salmon runs along the coast and king salmon of over fifty pounds are not uncommon (Nakalilok Bay on the Pacific side of the peninsula is particularly good and a record king salmon of seventy-five pounds was caught in the Kenai river in 1985), to Utah in the south where the Green river, part of the Colorado river drainage, yields good sized browns, rainbows and cutthroats. In one seven-mile stretch the trout have been measured at approximately 14,000 fish per mile, each averaging sixteen inches.

Other worthwhile destinations include Michigan's Au Sable river watershed which has 180 miles of brook, rainbow and brown trout waters; Oregon's North Umpqua River where thirty-three miles have been set aside for fly fishing and the river from Bridge Hole to Gordon Flow is the most celebrated water in all of the US for steelhead; Virginia's New river and Shenandoah for smallmouth bass, particularly the section from Bixler's Bridge to Foster's Boat Landing (bacterial infection possibly due to nutrient run-off from farming has affected older bass but good hatches in recent years are restocking the river in quantity); Montana's Armstrong's Spring Creek for browns and rainbows; Idaho's Snake River where Henry's Fork, near Last Chance, is often considered America's greatest trout stream, with steelhead and anadromous rainbow. The world record 39-pound kamloop rainbow was taken from Pend Oreille Lake in the north of the state. In Northern California the Fall river is full of huge, uncatchable rainbows the size of Zeppelins, but those around the one-pound mark are catchable, and much fitter than their equivalents in Britain. The Upper Delaware

River, only 150 miles west of New York, is part of American fly fishing history. The biggest fishing is in the main stem of the river which is dominated by browns, but if the levels are low (the river is regulated by dam releases) the trout migrate upstream, especially into the west branch.

Canada can offer spectacular wilderness fishing, British Columbia in particular, where the Skeena river, and its six major tributaries, particularly the Kispiox, are amongst the best places in the world to fish for native steelhead and the Elk river for native cutthroat. In Alberta, the Bow river downstream of Calgary is one of the best for trout, where twenty-inchers are frequently encountered.

Below: Fly fishing on Oregon's Deschutes river, one of the best trout fishing streams in the western USA, which flows for nearly three hundred miles from its headwaters in Central Oregon to the Columbia River. A wild run of steelhead starts at the mouth of the river in mid-July and by September Steelhead can be found all through the river.

Fly Fishing Around the World

There are a number of places around the world still on my list. One is the Kola Peninsula, roughly the size of Scotland, which lies in the far northwest of the Russian Federation, between the Barents Sea and the White Sea, and was originally closed to visitors because its strategic importance during the Cold War led to a proliferation of military bases there. Maybe as a result of such enforced isolation, over the last few years it has built up a reputation for some of the most prolific Atlantic salmon and sea trout fishing to be found anywhere in the world. Five different runs occur from May to October and the average fish run at twenty to twenty-five pounds.

Another on the list is the Himalayas, home to the mahseer, a huge fish of the carp family which takes the fly and which was a favourite quarry of the British in India in the 19th century. The major migration of the mahseer to their tributary spawning grounds is in the monsoon season of July and August when the rivers are full from rain and snow melt. After the end of the rains, as the waters recede, the fish return to the main rivers and are voracious. Mahseer have been known to top eighty-five pounds and plenty are caught around the twenty to forty pound mark – particularly when using a spinner. Substantial fish are still caught on the fly.

A five-foot taimen chokes trying to swallow a three-foot specimen, Mongolia, 2006.

Also high up my wish list is Mongolia for taimen, the largest species of salmon and trout family in the world. The current world record is just under a hundred pounds, though there have been reliable records of fish twice that size. The largest recorded, reportedly caught in the Kouty river in Russia, was nearly seven feet long and weighed just over 230 pounds. In 2006 scientists working in the Eg-Uur river basin in northern Mongolia found a five-foot-long taimen which had choked to death trying to swallow, head first, a three-foot-long taimen. They are apparently 'apex predators' in their river systems, but are endangered, so catch and release with barbless hooks is practised.

Fishing for salmon on the Falls pool of the Eastern Litza river, Kola Peninsula, northwest Russia.

Being Coarse

Coarse Fishing Lures

'Lure' is a broad term that includes any artificial object fitted with hooks used to attract and catch fish. In some areas where 'overbaiting' has led to ecological problems, lures are by far the soundest choice. Knotted to the end of the line they are designed to mimic the appearance and movement of fish prey. Lures can be manufactured from cork, plastic, wood, rubber or even metal. They can be designed to sink or float, to move swiftly through the water or much more slowly to resemble weak prey. A successful angler should have a range of lures to match different environments. Popular choices include:

Jigs One of the most versatile lures, jigs can be bought in all shapes and sizes and are regularly used in both coarse and saltwater fishing. They are controlled by the movement of the rod and are made of weighted hooks covered with attractive imitations of baitfish to get the fish's attention.

Above: A pair of spoons, suitable for light spinning.

Right (left to right): A heavier lure, the sort you cast a long way to get the big boys; a pike plug – note the adjustable diving vane at the front of the lure; a pair of classic lures that you could you use to catch anything from pike to sea bass; a light lure, one of the multi-purpose baits that you could use to catch just about anything.

Plugs Also known as 'crankbaits', 'deep-divers' have a wide lip which causes the plug to dive quick and deep when it is retrieved, whilst 'shallow-divers', with a much narrower lip, stay nearer the surface. The lighter 'floating plugs' are intended to look like surface swimming fish, whilst 'sinking plugs' explore deeper waters.

Spinners Distinguished by one or more propeller-like rotating blades designed to mimic the sharp darting movements of small fish with at least one hook at the other end. They are especially suited to areas heavy with weeds or murky waters. 'Bar spoons' have an egg-shaped blade, 'minnows' have a treble hook and resemble the minnow fish and 'spinnertails' are distinguished by their colourful tails which hang from one end and the spoon-shaped blade attached to the other.

Other Lures Thin and glinting 'spoon lures' are shaped like spoons, rubber or plastic 'bass worms' are often used, as are 'spinnerbait', pieces of wire bent at a ninety-degree angle with a hook on one end and a glittering spinner at the other.

A roach, with it's striking red-orange iris, is success-fully hooked.

Coarse Fishing in Britain

Above: *Communing with the river – touch ledgering.*

Opposite above: *Choosing a float.* Opposite below: *Chris Yates, champion angler (he has a 51-pound carp to his name) and writer, ledgering. Chris only ever uses spilt cane rods. For him fishing is 'like a high-pressure game of chess. Make the wrong move and it's checkmate, and the fish are changing the rules all of the time. If you do hook a fish and bring it in, there's nothing better, you can't transcend that moment…'.*

Previous pages: *A row of anglers enjoy an idyllic sunny afternoon beside a canal in the Loire Valley.*

The British Isles offer some of the best managed coarse fisheries in the world, despite the fact that roughly a million anglers use them, so we are spoiled for choice. The list that follows can do no more than hint at the possibilities, but it is a starting point – just don't forget that the UK is studded with stocked ponds and reservoirs which offer fantastic opportunities, even in the most unlikely places, far from the nearest river.

The Hampshire Avon is arguably the queen of all the river fisheries and the crème-de-la-crème is the Royalty Fishery, which offers just about everything, including double figure barbel, cracking chub, pike up to thirty pounds and carp up to nearly forty pounds, not to mention bream, tench, dace, roach and perch. The major hassle on the Royalty is coping with thick weed beds, but if the weed wasn't there, neither would the fish be and this is a venue every angler should visit once in his or her lifetime.

Lifelands Fishery at Ringwood on the Avon is another top water, which offers much the same opportunities as the Royalty, particularly big barbel and chub, and also bream, carp and dace, though not so many roach. Like the Royalty, there is always the chance of trout, sea trout and salmon. Staying with the Avon, the Recreation Ground at Fordingbridge has big roach and barbel; while the Town Water in Salisbury has roach, grayling, dace and chub for very cheap day ticket rates.

Moving farther afield, the Stour has some great fishing, particularly at Throop. The lower Stour competes with the Royalty as far as the quality of fishing goes, with barbel, chub, roach, bream and perch. This fishery is constantly in the angling news and must offer some of the best river coarse fishing in the country. Not so far away is Hatchet pond in the New Forest, which contains double figure big bream and has recently become known for its carp and tench fishing. The southwest has an embarrassment of riches as far as coarse fishing is concerned, and around Wimborne there is free water on the Stour full of big perch and roach.

The Thames, a river that older anglers will remember as a total write-off, is better now than it has been for perhaps the past fifty or sixty years, thanks to the combination of a huge conservation effort and an on-going environmental clean up. If you haven't been down to the river for a while, go, because in places it is now full of big trout, gigantic carp, barbel and perch, especially in the lower reaches. The Norfolk Broads have some tremendous fishing, particularly for bream, eels, perch, pike, rudd and tench. There are too many places

Clockwise from below: *What it is all about – the prospect of a day by the river…; a carp fishermans's 'bivvy', with a pair of legs just in view; throwing in bait balls to attract fish – these can be made of the most esoteric ingredients, often kept deadly secret; John Wilson, who used to present 'Go Fishing' on television, with a good sized carp; a good barbel caught on the worm in the Ouse in Yorkshire. The opening weeks of the 2007 season were particularly good with warm, high water with quite a few fish caught around the 8-10 pound mark.*

Coarse Fishing in Ireland

'The Anglers Rest' in Corofin, County Clare, where many a tale is told. As a warning, the Guinness advertisement above the door has the publican (an octopus) say to the punter 'Pull the other one!'. There is a good specimen of a stuffed human in a glass case on the wall.

The problem with writing about coarse fishing in Ireland is that there is almost too much choice – too many world-class venues to list in the space available. Much of Ireland's potential as a coarse fishing venue has yet to be properly explored. Ireland is far better known for its game fishing and until about twenty years ago, virtually no-one did any coarse fishing there – yet in recent years, the number of visitors has boomed and nowadays you are as likely to meet a German angler float-tubing for pike as you are to bump into a salmon angler. The slightly uncharted nature of Irish coarse fishing brings with it a new set of challenges for visitors, most of whom are used to being able to drop into the local tackle shop and pick up a leaflet to see what is available; while this is increasingly the case in Ireland, coarse fishing is still developing there and with a bit of luck it is quite possible to discover 'secret' waters. What follows are a few examples to tempt your imagination.

Near the top of the list must be the unfortunately-named River Suck, which flows along the boundaries of counties Galway and Roscommon – this is a very beautiful river, full of lily pads, enormous pike, roach, bream and tench. If the river is out of order, you can also visit the nearby lakes, such as Lough Loung, which holds bream, roach, rudd and pike.

The River Earn is described as 'Cavan's Golden Thread' and well it might be, because it is a fabulous river for roach and there are quite big trout in the higher reaches. If floods have transformed the Erne from its usual slow-moving state, Cavan has a lake for every day of the year, so you could fish it for most of a lifetime without having to visit the same location twice. Ireland offers literally thousands of lakes, many of which are free and Cavan has more than its fair share of them; if you want a base to operate from, you could want for little better than to stay near Kileshandra.

Ireland also has a canal system, which is where some of its best tench fishing is to be found and you could do worse than to explore the Royal, the Grand, and the canalized sections of the River Barrow. Tench

can also be found in Clare's limestone loughs and the lakes at
Carrickmacross in County Monaghan.

Roach are one of Ireland's big success stories, although they are not
native, having been introduced late in the 19th century. In many places,
they make up the bulk of the catch and they have turned up in some
surprising places, for example on the Cork Blackwater between Fermoy
and Mallow, which at one time was considered to be prime salmon
water, and still is.

Rudd, on the other hand, are as Irish as a pint of Guinness and can
be found in the loughs of County Roscommon and the magical lakes
around Corofin (at one time the inhabitants of Corofin couldn't agree
on how the name was spelt, so it appeared different ways at each end of
the town). Hybrids are quite a feature of Irish coarse fishing, the most
common being Rudd/Bream and Roach/Bream, and these can give a
good account of themselves, the river Barrow being a particularly good
spot for Rudd/Bream hybrids.

This picture was taken over the River Fergus, where it flows through the grounds of Clifden House at Corofin, aka 'The Gray House' in An Angler's Paradise by F. D. Barker, an American living in London, published in 1929. The book is an account of the author's experiences in Ireland, which he visited every year for long fishing holidays each May and September for two decades. In the book, Barker disguised his paradise by creating pseudonyms for the lakes and rivers, but Ireland is a small place and the location didn't stay secret for long.

The Cork Blackwater, with Ballyhooley Castle in the background, near Castletownroche. The river, which is about a hundred miles long, is one of the most important Irish rivers for coarse and game angling. Coarse fishing is particularly good in the Fermoy area where Roach and Dace abound.

Inset: An enormous pike caught in County Cavan. There are over three hundred lakes in Cavan, loosely joined by the River Erne, and they are a rich resource for roach, bream, tench and monster pike.

Coarse Fishing in Europe

Above: *Showing off a giant 86-pound wels catfish landed in Camargue, France.*

Opposite: *Sweden, like all the Northern European countries, is perfect for serious specimen hunters and recreational fisherman alike. The scenery's stunning too.*

I don't know why, but the word 'abroad' always brings up in my mind the headline 'Fog in Channel, Continent Cut Off', but while British fly fishermen have been travelling overseas since the 19th century, travelling coarse fishers have been something of a rarity until recently. There isn't any reason for this, because Europe offers more fishing than a single angler could explore in a long lifetime, but coarse angling tourism has only just started to take off as far as British fishermen are concerned and if you get going now, you will be able to say you were in at the start.

One of the locations that has to be at the top of any wish list is Telemark in Norway, where there is the chance of fantastic crucian fishing in the lakes, for fish running up to six pounds. Telemark is a fishing paradise, given that seven per cent of the landscape is covered by water and it has some of the most beautiful lakes in Europe. The Tana river in Finnmark gives anglers the chance of some absolutely huge grayling and while you are there, take a look at the map and see how much fishing the rest of this extraordinary country has to offer – there are 65,000 lakes with a surface area of over three and a half acres alone and most of them hold fish. The Norwegians tend to concentrate on promoting their game fishing and there have been some issues with restrictions on licences in the past, but the country has great potential as a coarse fishery.

The river Guden in Denmark flows through a land virtually unknown to British anglers, yet it is good for roach and bream, and catches of 100 pounds of roach in a day aren't impossible. The Danes are very keen anglers and this is one of the few countries where the vast majority of the revenue earned from fishing permits is channelled back into angling.

Travel west to the Loire in France and you can enjoy the local wine while you fish for barbel, carp, chub and pike. Another good French location is the River Tarn, which has lots bream, roach and carp, as well as pike, zander and catfish; while the nearby Dourdou has barbel and chub. Aveyron is also very good for chub and barbell. This area of France is reasonably off the tourist track, yet very beautiful and has enough good accommodation to make a combined family and fishing holiday a practical proposition.

Ice Fishing

Above: *Ice fishing in comfort, inside a fishing hut on Mille Lacs lake in Minnesota. Hut sizes varying from four holes and two bunks to twenty-two holes and twelve bunks can be rented by the twelve-hour shift or for the weekend.*

Following pages: *Thousands of South Korean anglers cast lines through holes of the frozen river in Hwacheon, seventy-two miles northeast of Seoul. The contest to catch trout is part of annual ice festival which attracted nearly one million visitors in 2008.*

The practice of fishing through carefully cut holes in frozen water has been around for thousands of years. Historically Native Americans used spears together with elaborately carved fish 'decoys', and fishermen in China leaned through the ice to secure their catches in nets.

Whereas in years gone by fishing through the winter was an economic necessity, today ice fishing attracts recreational and competitive fishermen and is growing in popularity every year, with annual festivals and championships drawing huge crowds. The US especially has seen participation rise to a level not seen since the 1960s. In some countries there are ice fishing resorts, complete with semi-permanent or even permanent fishing 'houses' that can be rented during the season.

Where Northern Europe: especially Scandinavia, Russia and the Baltic States. Asia: especially Japan, China, South Korea. North America: especially the northern United States and Canada

What Common species include perch, northern pike, trout, crappies (especially in North America) and walleye (native to North America and very similar to the zander). Ice fishing is particularly suited to catch and release. Fish need less oxygen to survive in the winter months because their bodies slow down and adjust to the colder temperatures. As ever, remember to handle your catch quickly and with care.

How At its most basic, ice fishing can be as simple as lowering your bait or lure to the bottom, raising it six inches or so and beginning a gentle upward jigging motion to attract fish. If nothing bites relatively quickly, you'll need to consider moving your position. Hi-tech gadgetry comes in very handy when picking a fruitful spot, but you can easily spend the day searching independently too – although digging many separate holes by hand will sap your energy. Another popular method involves the use of 'tip-ups' or flags attached to the end of the line which are raised when a fish bites. The line is retrieved by hand without the use of a reel. It's possible to set up a series of tip-ups in order to find the fish.

Equipment Ice fishing equipment can be as basic or as specialized as you choose. Many fisherman find warm clothes, a simple light jigging rod, a bucket to carry your baits or lures which can be upturned to provide a seat and some basic tools to cut your holes are all they need for a day's fishing. It is of course possible to spend much more on kit designed specifically for ice fishing with plenty of nifty gadgets available if you intend to spend a lot of time on the ice.

Basic checklist Ice auger (tool used to drill a hole in the ice); skimmer (tool resembling a slotted soup ladle used to keep the hole free from ice and slush); light jigging rod with a spinning reel; live bait and/or jigging lures bucket (which can double up as a stool); first aid kit; sensible clothes (the key is to wear layers to keep warm and dry – and take gloves and a hat); sun protection.

Below: Ice fishing huts of different sizes dot the surface of Mille Lacs Lake, Minnesota. Walleye and perch are the most frequent catches.

Advanced kit items Power auger: engine powered, making drilling holes quicker and easier. Especially good for cutting through very deep ice and making larger holes for bigger fish.

Ice fishing shelter a collapsible tent-like structure with a hard floor protects against the elements.

Fish finder or flasher a sonar unit which displays information including water depth and can let you know where fish are more likely to be found.

Underwater camera allows you to observe the fish's behaviour more closely and adjust your approach accordingly.

Safety It goes without saying that ice fishing can be dangerous. It's not something to try alone if you're inexperienced and don't know the area. It would be sensible to carry a mobile phone, GPS device and make sure that you leave details of your trip with someone before setting out. Adding ice picks to your kit is also a sensible idea in case you do get into trouble and need to get yourself back on the ice.

At Sea

At Sea

At one time, the sea was thought to be a limitless resource, a vast treasury that man could plunder without thought for the future, and how wrong that turned out to be. Sea fishing is a shadow of its former self, although the collapse of fish stocks has very little to do with rod and line fishing and everything to do with governments' lack of courage in regulating netsmen and so-called 'long-line' fishermen. Long lines are nothing to do with the kind of fishing you and I get involved in, consisting instead of miles of nylon to which hundreds of baited hooks are attached.

Once upon a time, sea fishing was a matter of trying to find enough weight to get your bait past the mackerel shoals fast enough not to hook them. You can still have days like that, but they are few and far between and catches are more modest than they were even in the 1960s, when it was possible to hire a boat and catch more cod than you could cope with. But if you have good advice there is great fun to be had all around the shores of the UK – and if you are prepared to travel farther afield there is literally a world to go at, from stripers off the Atlantic coast of North America to yellowfin tuna in Australia.

There are three main types of sea fishing: spinning for the predatory species, like bass and mackerel; bait fishing for deeper water fish, like cod and pollack; and wreck fishing, which demands specialist tackle and offers the challenge of tough fights with hardnuts like conger eels. You can even sea fish using a fly and recently more and more anglers have been turning to mackerel fishing using a fly rod. If you want a real challenge, you will need to travel, but with exciting opportunities on offer to catch tuna and marlin, there is the chance to pit yourself against some of the most powerful fish on the planet.

Most of us began our sea fishing careers the same way, jigging for mackerel, and even with the reduced numbers of fish in the sea these days, it is a fantastic way to introduce kids and adults who know how to enjoy themselves to the sport. You don't need much skill to jig for these attractive little fish, but for their size, they fight like tigers and they make good eating, as long as you don't catch too many of them. Once you have got the bug – and you will – it is time to move on, but most of the common species don't require specialist tackle and as long as you stay away from wreck fishing, you can do just about everything with the same rod. In fact, if you are very careful about soaking it clean so that the salt doesn't corrode the fittings and the reel, you can use the same kit to spin in a lake as you can for sea fishing.

At one time, cod used to be the prime quarry of sea fishermen in the UK, but overfishing has meant that numbers and sizes have plummeted and because cod don't have a tremendous amount of fight in them, you really do want to be catching a few to make it worthwhile. The most exciting of the smaller, non-specialist species are bass, which weight for weight are among the gamest things that swim and can put up the most tremendous fight on spinning gear, up there with the fittest trout or salmon you could wish to find.

While I think of it, the biggest secret among sea fishermen is that you can catch salmon in the sea. Salmon fishing in rivers is usually tremendously expensive, but it is a little known fact that salmon fight much better in salt water and there are many places around our northern coasts where they can be taken perfectly legally, with the added plus that you don't have to pay a penny for the privilege.

The trouble with fishing is that there is far too much to go at – how are you supposed to decide between being a fly, a coarse, or a sea fisherman? The answer is that if you are lucky enough to live in the UK, you can try 'em all without even having to travel very far; and if you do decide to travel, you will find you have a built-in ticket to the one of the most desirable clubs in existence, because fishermen speak the same language the world over. Go for it.

Rods and Reels

RODS

Sea fishing can be done by casting baits off the shore ('beach casting'), spinning, or fishing from a boat, and there are specialized rods for each method.

Beachcasters These are powerful rods designed to cast heavy baits a hundred yards or more and they vary from about eleven to fifteen feet in length.

Boat rods   Rarely used to cast any distance, these can be as short as seven foot six or less. Boat rods are classified by weight, rods rated less than ten pounds being suitable for small fish like mackerel and pollack, while fifty-pound class rods let anglers take on big species like shark and conger.

Grey's G-series 6 ft 6, 15–20 lb boat rod:
a bit light for hauling out conger, but would have a go at almost anything else.

Grey's Triplex 14 ft, 5 oz shore rod:
a beach casting rod for sea fishing along the wilder shores.

Grey's Platinum GSI 14 ft, 6 oz surf rod:
a powerful two section beachcasting rod. Light in weight, but it can hurl big bait a long way.

REELS

Multiplier reel This is the most popular type of reel for saltwater angling, because they have space for the enormous amounts of line which are necessary to play fish like sharks and marlin. The extra weight of the gear mechanism, considered a disadvantage by many fresh-water fly fishermen, is an advantage when sea fishing. These reels are sometimes designed to be used by anglers who are strapped into a 'fighting seat' and are placed above the rod handle so that there is room for both hands to grip the handle and take the strain of a big fish – which can be anything up to a thousand pounds.

Sturdy multiplier reels ready to tackle saltwater specimens lined up along the side of a chartered sea fishing boat.

Saltwater fly reel Designed to withstand the saltwater environment using manufactured aluminium, stainless steel and waterproof components to prevent corrosion. With bigger and more powerful fish to catch the spool is significantly wider in diameter than freshwater fly reels to allow for more line and backing. A powerful drag mechanism is also a must.

Bait casting reel Just as with coarse angling, the bait casting reel is for the serious angler using heavier lures and precise casts designed to catch big fish. The weight of the lure turns the spool during casting so the heavier the lure, the longer the cast – perfect for open waters – whilst the adjustable drag system can cope with a range of potential catches. Saltwater bait casting reels can also be used for other types of fishing.

Spinning reel Exactly the same as the freshwater reel, but the saltwater angler may benefit from the use of a skirted spool in which the drag mechanism is sealed. This allows longer casts, cuts down on tangles and affords increased line capacity as well as offering protection against the corrosive effects of saltwater.

Trolling reel This specialist sea fishing reel is designed to drag lures or bait whilst trolling in a boat.

Jigging reel Jigging reels are for casting a lure deep down then reeling it in using an up-and-down or side-to-side movement.

Bottom reel These are used for seriously deep fishing. They can be manual or even electric.

Natural Baits for Sea Angling

Sea Anglers can choose from a wealth of natural baits. The Irish Central Fisheries Board makes the following suggestions:

WORMS

Lugworm (*Arenicola marina*) The presence of this worm is recognized by the spaghetti-like spiral of sand they leave on the foreshore at low tide. Abundant in estuaries and on many sheltered beaches and trench digging for an hour or so with a garden fork will usually produce enough worms for a day's fishing. Traditionally a shore angler's bait, normally for flounder, wrasse, and dabs, but they are also very effective in attracting codling and whiting while inshore boat fishing. They can be kept alive for a few days, wrapped in newspaper and placed in a cool box.

Red and king ragworm (*Nereis pelagica* and *Nereis virens*) These are proven fish catchers and excellent bait for flatfish, whiting, pouting, codling and dogfish. They will stay alive for longer than a week if kept in a cool-box, on a tray of coral sand, and moistened regularly with fresh sea water.

Harbour ragworm or 'maddies' (*Nereis diversicolour*) Common in the muddy reaches of most estuaries. A bunch makes a good standby bait when float-fishing for mullet and wrasse or when ledgering for flatfish. Difficult to keep alive for more than a few days.

White ragworm or 'herringbone rag' (*Nephthys hombergi*) Fairly common in lugworm beds and effective in conjunction with other baits such as lugworm or mackerel strip, these will stay alive for up to a week if kept in similar conditions to red ragworm. However, white ragworm will not survive if put into the same tray as the more aggressive reds.

Large white ragworm or 'silvers' (*Nephthys caeca*) These are rare and localized in their distribution. They are, however, the single most sought after bait by shore match anglers and often the only bait that will attract fish in bright conditions. Many shore competitions have been won by the angler with a good 'silver' supply. Normally found in clean coarse sand in the vicinity of the low spring tide line. Large whites can be kept for quite long periods, in trays of moist coral sand, but should never be mixed with other ragworm species.

Top: *A worm hooked and ready to go.*

Middle: *The distinctive sediment patterns left by the lugworm in wet sand.*

Bottom: *A close up of the harbour ragworm.*

CRAB

Possibly the single most popular shore fishing bait, crab can be used in almost any sea angling situation. To ensure that crab baits are properly presented on the hook they should be tied on with elasticated thread.

The Common Shore or green crab (Carcinus maenus) moults at least once a year, usually prior to mating. This generally takes place in May or June, although it can be as late as October. They can be collected along sheltered shores but not all shore crabs are suitable as baits. The two most popular are "peelers" and "softies".

'Peeler crabs' These are crabs that are in the process of shedding their shells. To tell a "peeler" from an ordinary hard-backed crab, twist the last segment off one of the legs. If the segment comes away and there is white flesh underneath, the crab is unsuitable and can be returned to its hiding place. If, however, the segment comes away easily, revealing the newly formed, soft red flesh underneath, the carapace and under shell can be peeled off for use as bait.

'Softies' These are crabs which have already shed their shells but have not yet hardened (a process which takes about a week). They are rubbery to the touch and cannot nip as the claws are too soft to do any damage. In most conditions a soft crab will be almost as effective as a 'peeler', though the scent may not be as strong.

Hermit crab (Eupagurus bernhardus) can be collected in a pre baited drop net in rock pools or below pier walls. Hermit is good bait for cod, ray, and flatfish from boats, but is virtually impossible to cast from the shore due to the soft nature of the tail section.

Other species of crab such as the **velvet swimming crab** (Portunus puber) also make excellent baits but they are seldom encountered in moulting condition.

SQUID AND CUTTLEFISH

The **common squid** (Loligo forbesi) and **common cuttlefish** (Sepia officinalis) are superb baits. Squid will also fall occasionally to baited lures, while boat fishing and should be frozen while still fresh. They are well suited to being transported in a cool box, where they will remain frozen as long as the ice blocks are renewed regularly. Most tackle shops now carry the smaller **'calamari squid'** (Loligo vulgaris), which can be purchased frozen. These are valuable bait for various species of ray as well as dogfish, cod and conger.

Top: *A green shore crab in a rock pool.*

Middle: *The red hermit crab.*

Bottom: *A shoal of common squid.*

Top: *Cockles on the sand ready to be collected.*

Middle: *The common whelk.*

Bottom: *The shell of a European mussel lies on the beach.*

SHELLFISH

Shellfish are a very a valuable bait when fishing for specific species, particularly fish with soft or small mouths, such as haddock, sole or dab.

Cockle (*Cardium edule*) Cockles live buried just under the surface of damp sand. They are very useful for shore angling and inshore boat fishing and plaice, dab, flounder, whiting and all the wrasse family will take cockle freely. Cockle is also productive when used in a 'cocktail' with other baits such as lugworm or squid. Cod and whiting find this combination particularly attractive.

Common whelk or 'buckie' (*Buccinum undatum*) This is the largest of the whelk family and is tough bait for cod, whiting, pouting, coalfish, wrasse and dogfish. Common whelks are a deeper water shellfish than their cousins the periwinkles, living mainly among the stones and mud of the lower shore. As with hermit crab, a pre-baited drop net hung for a few hours at high tide from the end of a pier wall will usually yield ample whelk for a days fishing.

Common mussel (*Mytilus edulis*) Mussels can be found on most sheltered rocky shores, particularly near a fresh water outflow. Once removed from their shells, the soft flesh provides excellent bait for shore and boat fishing where codling, coalfish, plaice and dabs are expected. When not required for immediate use, they should be taken from their shells and frozen in batches of no more than twenty. Frozen mussels are an excellent standby for winter fishing when other baits are difficult to obtain.

Razorfish (*Ensis siliqua*) This is another excellent boat and shore bait, which is not uncommon but requires a little more effort to collect than mussels. Razors are narrow shellfish which grow to about six inches in length and live in damp sand near the low water line. They are difficult to dig because they can be up to three feet below the surface and the slightest movement on the sand sends them spurting to the bottom of their hole. The best method for capturing them is to take a carton of salt onto the beach, treading carefully onto the razor beds. Once a razor burrow has been located, some salt should be poured into the hole. In an effort to expel the salt, the shellfish speeds back to the surface, where they can be quickly grabbed and placed safely in a bucket. This can be a hit and miss exercise but an hour or so should yield twenty or thirty shellfish. Razor is tough bait, attractive to many species but particularly effective for bass and cod.

FISH

Oily fish is useful in virtually every sea angling situation, but is particularly effective when seeking the larger predators such as shark, tope, monkfish, skate and tuna.

Mackerel (*Scomber, scombrus*) Mackerel can be used as bait for almost every species of fish from both boat and shore. They can be used in 'strip' form for turbot, megrim, pollack, coalfish and gurnard, in 'last' form (the tough tail section) for ray, bull huss, spurdog and ling, or whole for sharks, skates and conger. Mackerel can be bought in most fish shops, in season, or can be caught while spinning from harbour walls or rocky outcrops. A string of brightly coloured feathers or lures can also be employed while boat fishing to take mackerel in numbers. Freshly caught mackerel will out-fish most frozen fish baits, but it is always worth stashing away a few fillets in the freezer for the leaner days of winter, when fish bait is scarce. Most oily fish deteriorates quickly, particularly in warm weather, and should be frozen within a few hours of capture. Mackerel can be frozen whole, but the innards should be removed and the stomach cavity cleaned out with salt water before doing so. Most local tackle shops now carry a supply of vacuum-packed frozen mackerel.

Herring (*Clupea harengus*) Herring are seldom caught on rod and line but are good bait for many species of fish. They can be bought fresh in most fishmongers and supermarkets and survive freezing better than mackerel – and do not deteriorate as swiftly when thawed. Herring works well in combination with other baits, particularly red ragworm.

Lesser sand-eel (*Ammodytes tobiannus*) This eel grows to about six inches and is a very important bait fish, excellent for bass, pollack, and dogfish. Common along sandy shores , they can be collected by the Cornish method known as 'vingelling' – that is, pulling a sweep in the top six inches of wet sand with a blunt bread knife or bill hook. When a sand-eel is located, it will wriggle out to the surface, where it must be swiftly grabbed before it can escape under the sand again.

Greater sand-eel or 'launce' (*Ammodytes lanceolatus*) The larger cousin of the lesser sand eel, the launce can grow to over a foot in length. It is a deeper water fish, seldom seen on the shoreline, but can be taken on small lures while boat fishing and is prime bait for turbot, ray, tope and cod. They will stay alive for several hours in a large bucket of sea water.

Top: *A razorfish scours the sea floor for prey.*

Middle: *Mackerel and herring – the perfect lobster bait.*

Bottom: *The greater sand eel peering out from its hole in the sea floor.*

Sea Fishing in Britain

Salmon fishing has beats, coarse fishermen have swims and sea fishermen have 'marks', so what follows is a sampling of marks around the British Isles. There are two main methods of sea fishing: beach casting and boat fishing. To have any chance of doing the latter most readers will need to hire a boat, but once you get connected, there are usually opportunities to pick up spare berths on day trips.

The northeast of England offers some great opportunities, starting with beach casting for big cod at Cullercoats, which is a well-known venue; just watch out for big breakers here, because the best fishing is from rock ledges and off the breakwaters. Blackhall isn't bad, either. Nearby Hartlepool has some of the best wreck fishing for cod in the country and Whitby is famous for boat fishing for haddock, coalfish, whiting, wrasse, pollack, and cod, with some occasional twenty-pounders being taken. Ling can also be had, as can saltwater catfish

A sea fishing lure which works well with bass.

and turbot if you are very lucky. On the northwest coast, St. Bees Head has some fine shore fishing which lasts more or less right through the year, and Northside beach at nearby Workington is good for flounder, plaice, bass and codling off the beach. Moving further down, Lowestoft and Corton in Suffolk are worth a trip, as is Skegness. In general the east coast lacks the wealth of species the south and west have to offer, but there is still lots of good fishing.

One of the prime southeastern marks is Dungeness, which offers great late summer and autumn fishing for bass, whiting, sole, flounder and dabs, together with cod in the winter. Big rods are needed, because you will need all the distance you can get and there are strong tides to contend with. If you fancy a bit of pier fishing, the Prince of Wales pier at Dover is worth a punt for mullet, sole, plaice, mackerel and all the usual stuff. Going round the coast, the Avon offers good sea fishing, as well as coarse and trout fishing – a cast off the beach can get you bass, eels, flounders, and dogfish, as well as winter whiting.

Without a doubt, the southwest is where the best fishing is to be had, and there are too many places to name, but Padstow has some of the best shark fishing in the British Isles, Ilfracombe has fantastic fishing of all types and the beach fishing in Cornwall has to be experienced to be believed. Wales also has some fine marks, with Aberdyfi being particularly good for bass in the summer. Scotland? Well, there is Rhue Lighthouse at Ullapool, which has superb Pollack and wrasse fishing out of deep kelp-filled ghullies; or Scrabster, which is a top venue offering ling, cod and pollock throughout the year, with scorpion fish, coalfish, wrasse and the odd bass off the reefs. Over the sand at Scrabster you can take dabs, plaice, turbot and flounder, as well as good spurdogs, and you have a reasonable chance of porbeagle shark.

Above: *At sea – into a big one?*

Below right: *No, just more mackerel.*

Left: *A good Pollack. Gut quickly and cook as soon as possible. They are becoming increasingly popular to eat.*

Below: *A good cast. Fishing off the beach at Seaton, Cornwall.*

Sea Fishing in Ireland

Ireland has a varied coastline, from the dramatic cliffs of the west to rocky shores and golden beaches. Just as its coastline varies, so does the sea itself, as Ireland's southern shores are heavily influenced by the warmer waters of the North Atlantic Drift, the boundary between the cold subpolar seas and the warmer subtropical currents. This makes for unlimited opportunities to fish for a huge variety of different species, and warm water fish more usual elsewhere such as amberjack, red bream, red mullet, blue shark, sunfish and triggerfish are often found in catches. There is also no close season.

Go down to Ballycotton in Cork and you can fish for mackerel, garfish, rays, flounders, bass, dabs, pollack, turbot, sole, plaice, codling, whiting and coalfish. The fishing is fantastic right across the bay, with dense mackerel shoals a problem at times – they make it difficult to catch anything else. There is also very good rock fishing off the islands such as Valentia in the southwest and along the coast of County Clare. Slea Head in Kerry has much the same variety of species off the beach; while Whiting Bay in Wexford has bass, tope, rays, plaice, dabs, turbot, dogfish and flounder, with an influx of whiting, dabs and coalfish in the winter. Bottom fishing for bigger species such as tope using fresh mackerel as bait is often fruitful in places like the Shannon estuary.

Deep sea fishing encompasses a wide variety: cod, pollack, coalfish, ling, conger, brill, turbot, tuna, halibut, haddock, gurnard, shark, ray and wrasse – over thirty species in all can be caught with rod and line. Deep sea fishing over wrecks can be very productive as wrecks attract fish, and large conger eels, ling, pollack and coalfish are the quarry here.

Big game fishing is a recent innovation, but not one which looks as if it is going to last. Albacore, or longfin tuna, arrive off the southwest coast of Ireland in late summer and have been caught for the last ten years or so (the record by Alan Glanville stands at 36.7 pounds – caught in 2003) but it was in 2000 that the first bluefin tuna succumbed to a squid-type rolling lure. Alan Glanville caught a 353-pound monster two miles out of Killybegs, off southwest Donegal, and then the very next day he caught one of 529 pounds, which took

A weever fish caught in the mouth of the Munster Blackwater at Knockadoon Bay. Stand on one of these fish, half buried in the sand with their venomous spines erect and you'll get a very nasty sting. The venom is deactivated by heat, so very hot water or towels should be applied as quickly as possible.

three quarters of an hour to get on board, and set an Irish record as the biggest fish ever caught on rod and line in Irish waters. That is until 2001, when a 968-pound leviathan was caught off Rahlin O'Beirne island, within three hundred yards of the shore. Since then many large fish have been caught but the numbers are now declining dramatically to the point where angling for them is probably no longer viable. Local fishermen put this down exclusively to the rapacious commercial fishing fleets. The EU commercial fleet has a quota of 23,000 tonnes but regularly catches more than twice that in mixed immature and adult fish. Scientists tell us that the mature stock in the North Atlantic is in the region of 50,000 tonnes. There is little or no control over bluefin fishing by the French and Spanish fleets, which regularly exceed their quotas without penalty. As things stand it is difficult to see how the stocks can recover, so unfortunately the bluefin may well disappear completely from Irish waters.

Above: *A typical mackerel boat long lining with feathers.*

Below: *Fishermen at dusk on the beach at Inch, Dingle Bay, County Kerry.*

Bluefin Tuna off Donegal
In October 2003 Adrian Molloy of Kilcar, the skipper of the Naomh Cartha, *took a scientist from Stanford University and two English anglers out to catch and tag bluefin. These images show them at work. Six months later the two tags turned up – one off Portugal and the other off the Bahamas – which proved that tuna stocks in the western and eastern Atlantic mix freely.*

Above: *A bluefin tuna jumps in the seas off Donegal, now a rare sight.*

Right: *the bait used: a surprised-looking squid.*

Above: Taking the strain of a 450-pound tuna.

Far Left: *The tuna is played out and comes alongside.*

Left: *A scientist has inserted a water hose to oxygenate the tuna's gills whilst the fish is tagged and a biopsy sample taken. The whole procedure was done as quickly as possible and the fish released.*

Fishing off the Great Barrier Reef, Australia

The Great Barrier Reef is the largest living organism on the planet, a colossal colony of limestone-secreting coral polyps stretching 1,430 miles off Australia's east coast, a complete living food chain, with the mass of coral providing shelter and food as predator eats predator. The national park surrounding the reef covers 128,960 square miles of ocean – an area roughly the size of Japan, in one third of which no fishing is allowed. Sailfish, barramundi, coral trout, yellowfin tuna, mahi-mahi, wahoo, cobia mackerel and giant trevally are the giants of the Coral Sea and estuaries of northeast Queensland, which has long been recognized as the black marlin capital of the world – where the marlin are twice as big as anywhere else. The area stretching from off Cairns (the closest major port) north to Lizard Island is regularly rated the number one game fishing region on the planet.

In November 2007 I had a chance to try my luck and joined the crew of a fishing boat skippered by the legendary Corey Hard in Cookstown on the northeast coast of Australia before cruising out to the Great Barrier Reef. Cookstown is briefly home to many of the crews that from each October spend three months working the Great Barrier Reef in search of the huge black marlin, which attracts fishermen from all over the world.

We would be living and sleeping on a mother ship anchored thirty miles offshore and inside the reef, which afforded some calmer water in the evenings. The routine was the same: after a hearty breakfast each morning we joined our crews in one of two fishing boats moored up either side of the mother ship. We would typically cruise out for ten minutes and then get eight rods overboard with a selection of lures, plugs and feathers to catch bait. Marlin can be caught using lures, but fresh bait is far more successful. It was never long before one of the rods bent over and the frantic winding began. In all honesty, there is not a great deal of skill involved in the catching of bait as it is down to the captain to get you in the right spot. If birds are feeding on the surface on krill, that is a good indicator of fish feeding below. As you sail through the mark you can often get six rods bent double in the space of seconds as fresh tuna attack the lures, and the solid muscle bulk of this fine little fish fights for its life. They usually run three baits in this part of the world with one small and two large sub-surface baits being trolled, so

Joining the marlin boats at Cookstown. My son Liam is closest to the camera and my business partner Adam Wheatley, who joined me on the trout fishing trip to New Zealand, is behind him.

Reaching the mother ship on the first night afloat.

quite a number of bait fish are required for a day's fishing – especially with the numerous opportunist attacks from other predators such as wahoo, which are never slow off the mark to spot a free feed.

With the bait on board we would power out to the fishing area and once the crew had rigged the hooks and sewn up the baits and weighted them, they would be trolled behind the boats at varying distances at about six knots, the optimum speed for catching marlin. At this point the captain would climb up into the tuna tower right at the top of the boat so he could observe the baits and also look for any other surface fish activity. On many occasions a marlin will follow bait for a few minutes, just holding off, as if to check its authenticity. Each fisherman will have been measured up for the fighting chair as we take it in turns in the seat. If you hear the captain shout 'on the centre' it means that the centre bait has just been hit by a marlin. Hit it they do, and as they do they create what is known as a 'hole', where the water is totally flat for a few seconds where the bait was. The bigger the hole, the bigger the fish. As your heart-rate quickens, there is a moment where nothing can be done but wait to ensure that the fish has indeed swallowed the bait and not dropped it. What follows is probably the most exciting sequence a game fisherman can experience, and it is what attracts so many to the

Above: *Waiting for the marlin to bite.*

Below: *She's on. Taking the strain.*

Opposite above: *Coming alongside, what seemed like hours later.*

Opposite below: *The last salute before letting her go free.*

In these two photographs you can see the marlin everting her stomach. This seems to be a natural process in order to expel the stomach contents. You can tell when a marlin is doing this because a foul-smelling oil slick full of half-digested fish appears on the surface.

with every sinew straining to try and win the battle. The technique is to stand in the chair and wind the two feet or so of slack line that creates. As you sit down again your body weight now against the tight line will move the fish upwards a foot and you stand again to wind in the slack you have created. This methodical 'pumping' of the fish may reap rewards, or, the opposite, bring on another reel-screaming run, leaving you contemplating the effort required to get the line back on the reel again. This can go on for literally hours, but it averages forty minutes for fish up to 500 pounds; much longer for larger fish. As the fish tires and nears the boat, the shouts of encouragement from the crew keep you from realizing just how hard your biceps and legs are working. At any moment you may feel the line go slack, telling you that the fish has escaped – or even been devoured by one of the many sharks patrolling below the boat. In that case your only trophy will be a massive, severed head and you can only imagine the weight and bulk of the beautiful fish that has eluded you. If you win, and the marlin comes alongside the boat, you may be lucky enough to see her jump again, in close proximity, to show you the huge girth and sheer scale of this majestic beast before the crew grab the leader and set her free.

As you try to stand or raise your arm to salute the skill of the crew you realize you can barely move as muscle fatigue sets in – but so does the most extraordinary, addictive, feeling of elation.

Above: *Pure elation, and physical exhaustion!*

Right: *A marlin boat with the crew in the tuna tower looking out for marlin.*

Opposite: *Another marlin jumps close to the boat. One, luckily not one of the biggest, jumped right into the boat, knocking over a crew member and thrashing around on the deck until we could get him out the side traps and into the sea.*

Following pages: *A heart stopping sight: a black marlin making its first leap at the end of a line.*

Fishing for Marlin off the Andaman Islands

The Andaman Islands are a chain of over three hundred islands – the peaks of a submerged mountain range – which link Sumatra in the south with Burma in the north, 450 miles west of Phuket in Thailand. The 3–6,500 metre drop off the east coast of Barren Island, 85 miles northeast of Port Blair, the capital of the Andamans, is one of the best fishing grounds for big fish. The Andaman's sit over a fault line (the sub-sea earthquake which triggered the giant tsunami of December 2004 was centred not far to the south) and Barren Island is an active volcano, with lava still flowing into the sea following the last major eruption about ten years ago. You can see the smoking cone and the lava in the photographs I took. The waters around the Andamans have never been commercially fished and because they are difficult to get to they are not on the tourist trail either – so they are a virtually

Right: *The* Red Hooker, *a Riviera 44, part of the* Wahoo *fleet: twenty knots top speed, fully air conditioned, the latest Shimano reels; a very comfortable boat.*

Opposite: *The volcanic cone of Barren Island.*

untouched marine ecosystem and a world heritage site since 2002. The result is that if a fish does not get eaten by a bigger fish, it tends to die of old age rather than from fishing, and that means in turn that the sizes they grow to can be enormous. Divers have spoken of seeing ten-foot-long dogtooth tuna, which would almost certainly be of world record size. Other fish which grow to bigger than average sizes include blue and black marlin, wahoo, sailfish, dogtooth and yellowfin tuna, dorado, giant trevally, groupers, narrow barred Spanish mackerel, swordfish, and sailfish. Bottom fishing produces big red bass, snappers and groupers, and fly fishing for barramundi and mangrove jacks around the coastal mangrove swamps is also on offer. The Andamans are altogether a fisherman's paradise. We opted to go for marlin and the photographs that follow show what happened.

Opposite top: *Where this lava now flows into the sea there was once a beatiful sandy beach.*

Opposite bottom: *The crater of the volcano on Barren Island, still smoking.*

Left: *The lines go over for baitfish. The crewman's T-shirt is being worn by my fishing partner, Sean O'Brien, and was printed for an earlier trip we did together.*

Middle: *A permit on board. They are strong fighters averaging ten to twenty pounds, but because of their shape no good as bait fish.*

Bottom: *Followed by a wahoo. Its long jaws with razor-sharp teeth show it is a predatory fish and allow it to rip into schools of squid and baitfish. When caught, wahoo make strong runs with abrupt changes of direction, sometimes leaping out of the water. This makes it one of the most exciting of the smaller game fish to catch. It is also a pest when fishing for marlin as it eats a high proportion of the bait fish.*

Following pages: *A pod of dolphins including a mother and calf play around the boat.*

Right: *A strike – and a black marlin is on and making a first jump. After a forty-minute fight she comes alongside,* below right, *before a final leap of defiance,* opposite page.

Following pages: *A blue marlin close up. The records for the largest blues are 1,402 pounds, caught in the Atlantic off Brazil, and 1,376 pounds in the Pacific off Hawaii (the black marlin record is 1,560 pounds, off Peru). Females grow to fifteen feet and weigh up to 2,000 pounds, but the males are smaller and grow only up to 400 pounds. They are extremely strong fighters and dive deep, make long powerful runs and head-shaking leaps. In the Andamans they fish with lures, while off the Great Barrier Reef they use fresh bait fish. Circle hooks rigged properly reduce injury risk and drop out after the line is cut.*

Spear Fishing

A blue water hunter in a kelp forest off of Catalina Island in the Channel Islands National Marine Sanctuary, California.

The Cosquer Cave, discovered in 1985 near Marseille, contains examples of cave art from the Upper Paleolithic period (between 10,000 and 40,000 years ago). Among the etchings are depictions of marine animals, most experts agree they are seals, being harpooned. Also mentioned in classical literature and the Bible, the centuries-old practice of spearing fish for food from beaches, oceans, shallow rivers and streams continues in many communities across the world to this day. In some countries it has evolved into an exciting, though sometimes controversial, extreme sport.

HOW IS IT DONE?

Whatever method you use, it's essential to approach the fish as quietly as possible. Dives should be made quickly and cleanly. Wearing a mask will distort your vision slightly – fish will seem closer and bigger than they are. With practice you will learn to adjust your aim to take account of this.

Wading The most traditional method, often done using a hand spear.

Shore diving This method, from beaches or headlands, allows you to explore reefs up to depths of around 80 feet.

Boat diving The best way to reach more remote areas like offshore reefs.

Bluewater diving This is defined by the International Bluewater Spearfishing Records Committee (IBSRC) as 'the capture or attempt to capture, with muscle powered speargun while breath holding and submerged, wild edible bluewater game fish species.'

WHERE?

Top locations for bluewater spearfishing include New Zealand, South Africa, Australia, Brazil and Mexico. UK waters too provide ample opportunities for spear fishing.

WHAT FISH?

Almost anything. Reef fish, tropical fish, game fish, freshwater fish… Reefs and areas with substantial rocky structures are the most fertile hunting grounds

EQUIPMENT

Whatever method you pursue you'll need to equip yourself with most of the following:

Hand spear With an elastic loop at one end and a sharpened point at the other.

Mask and snorkel It's imperative to make sure these fit perfectly. Some masks are more suited to shallow water, others give better visibility at greater depths.

Fins These should have long blades and, again, the fit is crucial as it can affect your ability to dive quickly.

Wetsuit This is imperative as spear fishing involves a lot of time in the water. The water temperature will help

Opposite: A blue water
hunter successfully captures
an elusive sea bass and
moves to secure it in his
keepnet.

determine the thickness of the wetsuit. Some wetsuits have extra padding around the chest, specifically designed with loading a speargun in mind.

Speargun The most important piece of kit. All spearguns are designed to be held and fired with one arm. There are two main categories: 'band' (elastic springs propel the spear) and 'pneumatic' (the spear is powered by compressed air). Pneumatic spearguns are extremely powerful but can be cumbersome to use and are more expensive. There are three further categories within band spearguns: 'Euro' (small and accurate over short distances, perfect for small fish, ideal for UK waters), 'multiple-band', 'wooden' (thicker spears, larger range, wooden handle, heavier – to combat the problem of recoil – the speargun for larger fish), 'hybrid' a combination (short barrel and wooden handle). As a very general rule, the clearer the water, the longer the speargun, but if diving amongst reefs or wrecks or exploring caves a shorter gun is much easier to handle.

Float Acts as a buoyancy and visibility aid and is useful as a means of carrying equipment.

Knife Essential for quickly securing a catch, but also for escaping from any tangles such as netting or kelp.

Fishkeep A means of securing any fish. It can be assembled easily using a sharpened steel bar and a strong cord which is attached to the float. A catch can be transferred to the fishkeep before the spear is removed.

SAFETY
A speargun is a potentially dangerous weapon. Never load or fire one out of the water and always handle with care – keeping the tip pointed away from your body and other people. Spear fishing, whether snorkelling or free-diving, requires a good level of general fitness and it is important to start slowly. A spear fishing organization will be able to provide you with all the practical information you need to get started safely.

ETHICS
Spear fishing for sport is generally heavily regulated. In the UK it is illegal both to spear fish in any non-tidal reaches and to profit from fish caught whilst spear fishing in the sea. It has been suggested that some species have been over-targeted, especially by bluewater freedivers, but it remains one of the most ecologically sound methods of fishing.

What not to Fish

Not all the fish you might come across on your adventures are harmless. Here are some to watch out for.

Barracuda (*Sphyraenidae* family)
Prized by big game anglers, different species of barracuda are found in the Atlantic, Pacific and Indian oceans. Large and physically powerful opponents, their long bodies sometimes stretch over six feet. Humans have sometimes come under attack from these fast and deadly predators with long needle-like teeth, with scuba divers the most common victims. Such attacks, however, are rare, and they are usually the result of the barracuda feeling threatened. Still, their size and force mean they should always be treated with caution.

Blue Ringed Octopus (*Hapalochlaena lunulata*)
Rarely topping five inches in length and weighing around two ounces, this tiny octopus is found in rocky pools and shallow coastal waters off Australia, especially around the Great Barrier Reef. It is light brown in colour – its startling deep blue rings only develop when it feels threatened. It feeds on small crabs and invertebrates, but will bite any attacker – even a human who is unfortunate enough to step on one. Its venom is highly toxic and there is no known antidote. Victims will experience breathing difficulties, severe nausea and possible paralysis. Immediate first aid followed by hospital treatment is vital if the victim is to survive. Without treatment within twelve hours the bite is usually fatal.

Above: The blue rings signify that the octopus has sensed danger – and could be ready to attack.

Right and following pages: Even without baring its razor sharp teeth the barracuda is a menacing presence.

Opposite: The electric eel makes its way along the river bed.

Decorated Rabbitfish or **Masked Spinefoot** (*Siganus puellus*)
One of the few venomous rabbitfish, this species is found around reefs in the Indo-Pacific oceans and nearly always travels in pairs. Bright yellow with a dramatic spotted black stripe extended across its eye, it is generally placid but when under attack it can use its extremely sharp and venomous dorsal fin spines to ward off predators.

Electric Eel (*Electrophorus electricus*)
In spite of its name, this carnivorous freshwater fish native to South America – especially the muddy bottoms of the Amazon Basin – has proved extremely difficult for scientists to classify with certainty. It actually comes closer to a catfish than an eel, and is not a member of the eeel family though it shares many of their physical characteristics – the electric eel has an powerful elongated body, murky colouration and is without scales. Electric organs on the abdominal portion of its body contain around six thousand 'electrolytes', minute cells that store

power. When hunting or defending itself from attack, the electric eel can release all this electric charge, sometimes in excess six hundred volts. Injuries to humans as a result of an encounter with an electric eel are very rare, but multiple shocks can cause a person to go into cardiac arrest. Deaths by drowning have also been reported after victims were incapacitated by electric eels.

Moray Eel (*Muraenidae* family)
Found worldwide in the shallow reefs of temperate and tropical waters, there are almost two hundred different species of moray eel. The giant moray can reach ten feet in length, but the average size is little more than half that. Like the other members of the eel family, morays are without scales and slimy in appearance. The most remarkable feature of the moray is its jaws, which are large and filled with sharp, almost canine teeth to snare prey. The narrowness of the moray eel's head makes it difficult to swallow their catch, but to overcome this, they use a second set of jaws, known as pharyngeal jaws, which are positioned inside their mouths. These are lined with teeth and take on the responsibility of maneuvering their catch so that it can be digested. The moray's fearsome teeth make it dangerous to humans, but attacks are rare and usually don't occur without some sort of provocation.

Top: *The red-bellied piranha – one of the deadliest species around.*

Bottom: *Its vivid coloration makes the decorated rabbitfish an aquarium favourite – despite its venomous fin.*

Piranha (*Serrasalmidae* family)
The pirhana's ferocious set of pointed interlocking teeth and its reputation as a committed carnivore capable of stripping flesh from bones in seconds has made it one of the most feared fish in the world. Yet the truth is a little less hysterical. Only four or five of the forty or so species of freshwater piranha fish (all of which are native to the Amazon Basin) pose a risk to humans, and most are just as happy eating insects and plant matter as they are devouring meat. That said, there is a risk, particularly to swimmers. They are also a popular target of adventure fishermen, who lure them with tempting meaty baits, but great care must be taken to avoid those teeth when reeling one in. In recent years Piranhas have increasingly been found in unusual places – often as a result of illegal trade. In 2004 one of the most fearsome species, the red-bellied piranha (*Pygocentrus nattereri*) was found in the River Thames, and in 2006 a Stockport schoolboy caught another in his local pond. In both cases the piranhas were thought to have been released by their owners.

Top: *A man-o-war spreads its tentacles whilst floating in shallow water.*

Bottom: *A red lionfish swimming on a reef.*

Opposite: *The terrifying jaws of a great white shark.*

Portuguese Man-O-War (*Physalia physalis*)

So called because its distinctive blue-purple air bladder resembles the triangular sails of 16th-century Portuguese ships, this complex creature looks like a jellyfish but is actually a siphonophore – a colony of three separate marine species that cannot exist independently. Its venomous tentacles are usually around three feet long, but can grow to as much as thirty feet. A common sight in tropical and subtropical regions of the Indo-Pacific, they move with the tides and in recent years several have been washed up on British beaches. A sting is extremely painful and in isolated cases has proved fatal – though in general, swift first-aid treatment will prevent the venom travelling around the body.

Red Lionfish (*Pterois volitans*)

The red lionfish is a member of the scorpionfish family (*Scorpaenidae*) native to the reefs of the Indo-Pacific. Known by a variety of common names (including turkeyfish, zebrafish and red firefish) this brightly coloured species preys on small fish, crabs and shrimp, using its venomous dorsal spines to stun its target. The spines can be lethal to humans too, but swift treatment usually ensures survival – though the stings are said to be extremely painful. Popular aquarium fish, they have recently been found in Atlantic waters around the United States and their numbers are on the rise.

Shark (*Selachlmorpha superorder*)

The rate of shark attacks on humans is increasing steadily year on year, though experts suggest this can be explained by the simple fact that humans are spending increasing amounts of time in the sea. Three species are responsible for most of the attacks: the great white shark (*Carcharodon carcharias*), tiger shark (*Galeocerdo cuvier*) and bull shark (*Carcharhinus leucas*). The much-mythologized great white can reach up to twenty feet in length and is found worldwide, largely in temperate waters. It is a voracious predator, and it is thought that its attacks on humans are often the result of mistaken identity. The enormous diversity of shark species in the sea make them popular targets among sea fishermen, but theirnumbers are on the decline.

Stingray (*Dasyatidae* family)

Found worldwide in saltwater and in freshwater in Asia, Africa and the Americas, stingrays stick to shallow tropical and temperate waters. Despite their distinctive shape they can be difficult to discern as their flattened bodies are often concealed on the sandy bed. They feed on small fish and bottom-dwelling invertebrates. Venom is contained in barbed spines located along their tails. In general they are not aggressive; they react by violently whipping their tails only when disturbed by predators or humans. Most human victims of a stingray barb are wounded in the foot, but in September 2006 television naturalist Steve Irwin suffered a fatal barb to the chest whilst snorkeling on the Great Barrier Reef. It is thought Irwin was swimming too close to the ray which consequently felt threatened by his presence. Stings are painful, and every victim should seek medical attention as the barb breaks off once a sting has been administered the wound should be thoroughly cleaned.

Top: *A stonefish fully camouflaged.*

Bottom: *A greater weever fish moves along the sea-floor.*

Stonefish (*Synanceia verrucosa*)

Another member of the scorpionfish family (*Scorpaenidae*) and the most venomous fish in the world, the stonefish is found in the shallow and tropical waters of the Indo-Pacific. Despite their size – on average they are ten to fifteen inches long – their ability to camouflage themselves among coral reefs and rocky beds makes them incredibly difficult to spot. The stonefish's protein-based venom is contained within the thirteen spines that line its dorsal ray, and causes its victim to go into deep shock, somtimes resulting in paralysis. A deep wound can be fatal unless treatment is received and the venom successfully isolated within hours. The pain of a stonefish sting is said to be unbearable, and some victims have had to have limbs amputated following an attack.

Toad Fish (*Batrachoididae* family)

There are sixty-nine species of toadfish worldwide in fresh, brackish and saltwaters. Their name is derived from their toad-like appearance – they are dull in colour, without scales and have disproportionately large heads and prominent mouths. The two species to watch out for are native to Central and South America. The *Thalassophryne* and *Daector* both possess extremely sharp and venom-injecting spines on their dorsal fin and gill covers. They typically inhabit sandy and muddy sea or river bottoms.

Left: *A southern stingray glides along the sea bed.*

Below top: *The Toadfish emerges to search for prey.*

Below bottom: *This one should be familiar to film fans – Bubbles from* Finding Nemo *was a yellow tang.*

Weever Fish (*Trachinidae* family)

The eight species of weever fish, with venomous spines on both their gill covers and dorsal fins, are found in the North Atlantic and Mediterranean. It's the brownish lesser weever fish (*Trachinus vipera*), which favours sandy shallows, that poses the most danger to humans – especially bathers and shore anglers. They have been spotted all around the UK coastline. The risk of stumbling upon a lesser weever, which rarely exceeds four inches in length, increases at low tide and during the balmy summer months. Again, wounds are most likely to be inflicted onto the soles of the feet and whilst they are painful they are not considered life threatening.

Yellow Tang (*Zebrasoma flavescens*)

Found around the reefs in the warm waters of the Indo-Pacific, the yellow tang is one of seven species of *Zebrasoma*. Its oval body, pointed snout, prominent sail-like fin and vivid yellow colour make it attractive as an aquarium fish, but it requires extremely careful handling due to the scalpel-sharp spine on the base of its tail, which is used to slash anything that threatens to encroach on its territory. Even a tiny tang can cause a wound that will require a hospital trip. The regal tang (*Paracanthurus hepatus*) and the blue tang (*Acanthurus coeruleus*) possess the same razor-like tail spine.

The Future

We live in interesting times. In this era of rising energy prices, global warming and widespread unrest, all the old certainties have been overturned. What was once good, is now bad – to take but one example, farmed fish, which were once promoted as a resource to save the planet, have turned out to be an ecological disaster that governments find it hard to turn their backs on. Some hard choices are going to have to be made and sea food, which is such a healthy option, carries with it the burden of over-exploitation – for instance, shark stocks in the North Atlantic have managed to fall by at least fifty per cent in the past thirty years, without anyone noticing until recently.

Does any of this matter? Should we, as rod and line fishermen, worry about what commercial fisheries are doing to the seas around us? I think so; in fact, I believe so very passionately, because if we do not argue for the welfare of fish, who else is going to stand up for them? Certainly not the crews of the ocean-going factories that ingest entire shoals and process them into fish steaks for microwave dinner eaters. Fish ain't cute and they ain't cuddly and although it might seem ironic that people who take pleasure in catching them might also have an interest in preserving them, isn't that the bottom line of all hunting? If, as a hunter, you do not love your quarry and fight to preserve a breeding surplus, there won't be any to catch tomorrow and you will surely starve because you stupidly failed to manage your resources. People who buy fish in a supermarket don't get the opportunity to hold the living animal in their hand the way we do, and neither do they get the chance to think about it, the way we must, if we are to continue to enjoy our sport.

One way around this is stocked fish. After some early problems, put and take fisheries have got their heads around the issues and run environmentally friendly operations that never make the headlines because they make their money out of stocking fish at a density that makes them just hard enough to catch to be interesting. Sure, you do hear the occasional horror story about some of the new breed of trophy coarse fisheries, but if anglers in general make it clear that size isn't everything, the numbers game will take a back seat and the sport will be better for it.

Catch and release has a bad name in some circles, partly because there are those who maintain that releasing fish plays into the hands of people who are against angling, the argument being that it makes it clear that we are fishing for sport, not food. But to say that is to forget the legions of coarse anglers, who routinely release everything they catch and have done so for decades without losing the comfortable image of dad snoozing under his umbrella – and that is despite the fact that dad is awake these days and has five grand's worth of state-of-the-art kit at his side. Fishing has moved into the digital age and our attitudes need to move with it; there is a great deal of evidence that catch and release has made a big difference to Scottish salmon catches, and if we are going to leave this planet a better place for our children, conserving fish stocks is a great place to start.

More than anything else, though, if we want our kids to enjoy fishing, we need to take them fishing. So many parents are content to bring up a generation of couch potatoes, who need to be surgically removed from their consoles before you can even have a conversation with them, when there is everything to play for out there. Take a young lad or lass out and get them stuck into a big carp, or a five pound trout, and you give them a window into a world that many of them will never have suspected existed, a sport full of the most fantastic moments.

I should know, I'm a fisherman.

Glossary

AFTMA
The America Fishing Tackle Manufacturers' Association, which sets standards for some types of fishing tackle, including fly lines.

Anadromous fish
A fish that spawns in fresh water, but lives in salt water, the salmon being a good example.

Anglers' curse
Caenis flies, because fish love them and they are so small they are impossible to imitate.

Antron
A synthetic yarn used for tying flies.

Bail arm
A part of a fixed spool reel which revolves to wind the line onto the spool.

Back-cast
The action of throwing a fly line backwards with the rod.

Backing
Thin nylon or Terylene thread used to provide extra line to play a large fish with, when it has run the entire length of a fly line off the reel.

Bait
Natural attractant added to a hook to catch fish. Bait includes live and dead baitfish, crabs, crayfish, worms, eels, insects, mussels, clams, cut bait (fish), chicken livers, corn kernels, dough balls, squid, and shrimp.

Bag limit
The maximum possible number of fish that can be taken from a piece of water in a single day.

Barb
A backward pointing spike on the point of a hook, that makes it more difficult for a fish to wriggle off the hook.

Bead-head
A fly tied with a metal bead pushed onto the hook.

Beat
An identified length of bank along which a fisherman can expect sole occupancy.

Bite alarm
A device which alerts an angler to a take by a fish.

Bivvy
An open-fronted shelter used by some fishermen, particularly carp anglers.

Blade Bait
A weighted, fish-shaped blade made with a swinging hook and designed for fishing deep.

Bobbin
A tool for holding fly-tying thread.

Breaking strain
The amount of weight that can be put on a line before it snaps.

Buzz bait
These 'safety pin' wire lures for surface fishing have a propeller blade on one wire and a weighted body, skirt and hook on the other.

Buzzer
Any chironomid (midge) imitation.

Caddis
Any sedge fly imitation.

Caenis
A very small fly which often hatches in huge numbers. Caenis are so small and so numerous that fishing becomes almost impossible when they are about.

Cape
The area of feathers between the nape of the neck and the shoulders of a bird bred to produce fly tying feathers.

Caster
A maggot that has pupated.

Casting spoon
A spoon-shaped metal or hard plastic lure that wobbles to attract fish. They can be fitted with a fixed (solid) hook or swinging hook, that has a single, double or treble points.

Chenille
A furry material which comes in long lengths and is used to tie some flies, mainly lures.

Chumming
A fishing technique by which bait or scent is released into the water to attract fish to take a lure or baited hook. Chum consists of live, dead, ground-up or prepared baits and scents and is used in fresh and saltwater.

Cinch knot
A knot used to tie the leader to the hook.

Coarse fish
Any fish that isn't a salmon, trout, or grayling.

Crank bait
A fish-like hard lure or plug designed to swim under the surface, often made of plastic or wood. Some are combined.

Cul-de-canard
Feathers taken from near the preen gland of a duck. These are coated with a special oil and float incredibly well.

Dapping
A method of fly fishing which involves using a very long rod and line which is blown about by the wind, so that a single fly tied on the end literally dances across the water.

Dead bait
A dead fish used as a lure.

Deer hair
Sometimes used for tying floating flies.

Disgorger
A tool used to get the hook out of the mouth of a fish without injuring it.

Double-Spey cast
Beautiful to watch, if well done. The cast starts with the fisherman drawing the line across the water in front of him, then the rod tip is swept back in order to form a loop beside the angler and the cast finishes by rolling this line out across the water. A master can cast a phenomenal distance with very little effort.

Drogue
A bag of plastic, or sometimes canvas, that is towed from a boat in order to slow its rate of drift down.

Dropper
A length of nylon standing out at approximately right angles to a fly leader, to which an additional fly can be attached in addition to the one on the tip of the leader.

Dry fly
A fly which is fished floating on the surface of the water.

Dubbing
Material wound around the thread used to tie artificial flies.

Dun
An adult insect which has just emerged from the nymphal stage and is capable of free flight.

Elk hair
Similar to deer hair.

Emerger
An aquatic insect in the process of making the transformation from nymph to dun – they emerge through the water surface, hence the term.

False cast
A cast made by a fly fisherman for the purpose either of drying the fly, changing the angle of the cast, or letting out more fly line.

Fighting chair
A swivelling chair bolted onto the floor of a deep sea fishing boat into which an angler is strapped with a harness so he can fight big fish.

Fixed spool reel
A reel designed for spinning or bait fishing, one of the chief features of which is a spool that does not revolve as line is paid out or retrieved.

Float
Also called a 'bobber' in the US, these suspend hooked baits off of the bottom, and signal hits by 'bobbing' when a fish takes the bait.

Floatant
A chemical applied to a fly in order to make it float.

Floss
A broad thread, usually synthetic, but sometimes made of silk, used for tying flies.

Fly
An imitation of a living creature, usually an insect, created by tying feathers, fur and man-made materials around a hook in order to fool a fish into thinking it is something edible.

Fly reel
A reel designed for fly fishing.

Foul hook
Catching a fish somewhere other than in the mouth.

Fry
A very young fish, usually just hatched.

Game fish
Usually refers to salmon, trout, or grayling, but sometimes used to include salt water species.

Ghillie
A Scottish term for someone, generally a fishing expert, who, like a golf professional, is employed to help and advise.

Grilse
An Atlantic salmon which has only spent one winter at sea. These fish are usually seven pounds or less.

Groundbait
Anything edible thrown into the water to attract fish.

Hackle
A feather used for fly tying.

Hatch
The appearance of many duns on the water, as nymphs come to the surface in order to complete their transformation into winged adults.

Hook
A metal wire device shaped like a 'J' with an opening or 'eye' at one end to which the line is tied and a point at the other end to catch the fish. Circle hooks have an angled point. Double and treble hooks have two or three points, respectively.

IGFA
International Game Fish Association.

Jig
Sometimes called 'bucktails', these weighted-body (often lead) lures are moulded on special hooks and rigged with a hair tail or soft plastic skirt or worm.

Jigging
A method of dropping a lure into the water over a fishing site and moving it – 'jigging it' – up and down to attract fish. Done from a pier or boat.

Keeper/keeper ring
A ring found near the butt of a rod, which is used to hook a fly, or bait onto, so that the line doesn't get tangled when it is being transported.

Keepnet
Used by some coarse fishermen to keep fish that they have caught, before releasing them later. Banned by many fisheries, but essential for most competitions.

Kelt
A salmon that has spawned and is falling back towards the sea. In the case of the Atlantic salmon, less than one in ten makes it.

Landing net
A net used to lift a fish that has been caught out of the water.

Leader
A length of monofilament, wire or other stranded material tied between the end of the line and the lure or hook. Leaders provide extra strength or abrasion resistance from the rough mouth and teeth of fish (pike, barracuda, sharks), scales (sharks), gill covers (tarpon and snook), blows from tails (tuna).

Ledgering/legering
Fishing any bait on the bottom without a float. A weight of some kind is normally used.

Lie
A place where a fish rests and feeds.

Line
Specialized 'string' used for fishing. Nylon monofilament line is the most popular. Other lines are made of different materials, including braided fibres and wire. FLY LINE is a specialized line made of a plastic coating on a core, and often made tapered (changing diameter) to make fly casting easier.

Loch-style fishing
Fly fishing from a boat, using long leaders with several flies attached. The line is cast out, retrieved and then lifted slowly, so that the flies dance along the surface until the back cast is made.

Lure
Any artificial item designed to attract fish and fitted with hooks. These include flies, hard plastic or wood lures (or plugs), soft plastic imitations, large offshore skirted baits, metal spoons, lead-head lures (jigs), bladed lures, spinners, spinnerbaits.

Mark
An area of the sea which holds fish.

Match fishing
A coarse fishing competition.

Mayfly
In the UK, one of the big upwinged flies from the genus *Ephemera*, in the US, the term includes the ephemeroptera as well – in other words, all the upwinged flies.

Mend
The action of throwing a curve in a fly-line in order to compensate for different speeds of water flow.

Nail knot
A knot used to connect a leader to a fly line. Sometimes tied with a nail, hence the term.

Nymph
The larval form of aquatic insects.

Parr
A young Atlantic salmon in its river-living phase. They spend up to three years in their home river before going to sea as smolts.

Pattern
Another word for an artificial fly.

Peg
The place at which a match fisherman sits, usually drawn by lot and marked with a peg, hence the term.

Point
The fly at the very end of the leader.

Pool
A place on a salmon river where fish lie. Pools are usually relatively deep and slow-flowing and have a head, into which the water flows, and a tail, out of which the water exits.

Pitch
A place where a coarse fisherman sets up his gear to fish.

Quiver tip
A very sensitive tip fitted to the end of a coarse fishing rod to help the angler detect bits.

Reel
A mechanical device for holding and spooling fishing line. Reels have a line spool, brake to slow running fish, handle to retrieve line and foot for clamping to a rod. Reel styles include CASTING (revolving spool), SPINNING (line coiling off stationary spool); SPINCAST, (like spinning but with a nose cone), and FLY (storing thick fly line/backing and to fight big fish).

Redd
A scrape in the gravel on a river bed created by a hen fish about to spawn.

Retrieve
The act of recovering line.

Rise
The disturbance in the water made by a fish coming to the surface. It can vary from a set of rings, to an enormous splash.

Rod
A long lever, usually made of fibreglass, graphite or composite materials and used to catch fish. Different types are available, such as rods for spinning, fly fishing, spincast, bait casting, boat fishing, offshore trolling, surf fishing, jetty/pier fishing, etc. Most rods have a reel-holding clamp and guides through which the line runs.

Rod rest
A device used by coarse fishermen to support their rods clear of the ground.

Roll cast
A cast made by flicking a stationary fly line out without the line going behind the angler.

Run
A stretch of relatively fast water between two pools.

Sea trout
A brown trout that spends some of its life at sea.

Sedge
A type of aquatic insect – known in the US as caddis.

Shooting head
A specialized fly line designed for distance casting.

Shot
Dense metal balls attached to nylon to make it sink, or to weight a float.

Single-Spey cast
A fly fishing cast rather like a roll cast, but which is started by pulling the line across the water towards the angler.

Sinkant
A chemical preparation applied to a fly to make it sink.

Sinker
A weight of lead or other metals designed to sink a hooked bait or lure.

Sink-tip
A fly line which floats, apart from the last few feet.

Smolt
An Atlantic salmon which is in the process of going to sea for the first time.

Snap
A small device similar to a dog leash snap, tied to the line and used for attachment and quick release of hooks, rigs and lures.

Soft plastic lures
Made of a soft plastic to resemble a worm, lizard, crayfish, shrimp or generic wiggling creature. Often sold in bulk to be rigged on a hook by the angler.

Specimen
A particularly good fish.

Spade-end hook
A hook which has a triangle of metal flattened at the end of the shank, instead of an eye, which is more normal these days.

Spinner
An artificial bait. Spinner blades rotate around the straight wire shaft of these weighted lures. Also a female aquatic insect which has returned to the water to lay its eggs.

Steelhead
A migratory rainbow trout, found in the US and Canada.

Still Fishing
Fishing without moving the bait once it is cast with replaceable soft plastic tails.

Stocked fish
A fish reared by man for the purpose of being released into a fishing lake or river.

Strike
Any 'hit' by a fish taking a lure or bait. Also the action of setting the hook initiated by the angler sweeping the rod tip back.

Structure spoon
Both casting and vertical jigging techniques are used for fishing these swinging hook heavy metal lures.

Swim
An area of water which holds 'coarse' fish.

Swivel
A small device with two or more eyes (rings) a central swiveling part. They are used between a lure or leader and line to prevent line twist. Otherwise, line twist can occur when a revolving lure twists line to cause tangles.

Tackle box
A box or bag with special compartments and features to hold terminal tackle, lures, hooks, and other fishing gear.

Take
The moment a fish takes a fly, or bait.

Terminal tackle
A general term for describing bobbers, sinkers, hooks, rigs, snaps, swivels and other gear used at the end of a line.

Terrestrial
Non-aquatic insects taken by fish, for example, beetles and grasshoppers.

Test curve
The weight needed to make a rod tip bend at an angle of ninety degrees to the butt. Applies to coarse and sea fishing rods.

Top water lure
Lures made of hard plastic, wood, hollow rubber/plastic and designed to float on the surface to attract fish when twitched or moved.

Trolling
A method of slowly running a boat while trailing lures or bait. This fishing method is used to cover a lot of water and to find fish.

Trolling spoon
A large spoon that is trailed, or trolled, behind a boat to catch fish.

Trotting
Allowing a float to go down river at the same speed as the current.

Tube bait
Made of soft plastic, these tubular lures are fished with special weighted hooks inserted into the hollow body.

Vice
(Vise in the US) a tool used to hold the hook while a fly is tied on it.

Weedless spoon
Wobbling spoons made with a fixed hook and guard for fishing weeds.

Wet fly
An artificial fly which is fished beneath the surface.

Acknowledgements

Above: *On board a marlin fishing boat off the Great Barrier Reef with my Olympus ready to record the action.*

Opposite: *Pinot at play*

A book of this scope could not have been written without a great deal of help from a variety of people. I am a fly fisherman by preference, though have dabbled in the past in coarse fishing, and have done a bit of sea fishing – particularly game fishing – so my knowledge is a bit sparse in some of the more arcane areas, particularly in coarse fishing where so many specialist clubs have flourished and grown over the last few decades. I am extremely fortunate because, as a cricket commentator, I get to visit exotic places all over the world like the West Indies – where I have been fishing with my old rival and great friend Viv Richards – India, Pakistan, Australia, South Africa and New Zealand in particular, and in between test matches I can take time off to sample the local fishing. And I will continue to do so!

The first person I must thank for helping to create this book is Andrew Herd, our consulting editor, who seems to have fished all over the world in every water imaginable, and whose knowledge about the detail of equipment, of rods, reels, bait, lures, flies and so on is unsurpassed. His book *The Fly: Two Thousand Years of Fly Fishing* is fascinating reading and has also been posted on the internet (http://www.flyfishinghistory.com), where it has grown every year in size and scope since it was first posted eight years ago. Andrew is also a very competent photographer and has taken many of the images in this book, very many specifically for the technical sections. He spent long hours helping on every aspect of this book.

Richard Sanderson, the managing director of Hardy and Greys Limited (http://www.hardyfishing.com) the incomparable manufacturers of some of the world's finest fishing tackle, has been extraordinarily helpful. He selected the cream of the Hardy's range and got it driven a considerable distance to Andrew Herd's studio to be photographed. Very many thanks, Richard.

Jon Ward-Allen, the editor of *Waterlog* magazine (which describes itself as 'the world's finest angling magazine – humourous, witty incisive, eccentric, unique, informative, passionate, inspired, political, intelligent and conservationist…'), and owner of The Medlar Press, a publisher of classic and modern and beautifully produced books about fishing, kindly allowed us to use his archive of photographic images (http://www.waterlogmagazine.com and http://www.medlarpress.com).

Chris Yates, author of *How to Fish*, *Passion for Angling* and *Casting at the Sun* and other seminal books (and a former British record holder with a fifty-one-pound carp from the famous Redmire Pool) was very helpful in suggesting coarse fishing locations, which I know little about.

To Olympus, who provide me with my cameras, without which some of the more dramatic fishing images in the southern oceans would not have been possible. I used my trusty Olympus cameras and their magnificent lenses (*opposite*) to take many of the photographs in this book.

To my dog Pinot (*below right*), a Parson's Jack Russell who is my faithful companion on all my fishing trips in Britain. He particularly enjoys the packed lunches.

To my son Liam and friend, agent and business partner, Adam Wheatley, both experienced and passionate fishermen, who have shared many of my adventures.

To the staff at Weidenfeld & Nicolson a huge thank you. To Michael Dover, my publisher and editor, for suggesting the book in the first place. From a standing start I think he could now take on anyone in a pub quiz about fishing… to Brónagh Woods who also spent long hours putting the book together, to Clive Hayball who created the design, to Debbie Woska, Jennie Condell and all the other members of the team, my grateful thanks.

To my wife Kath, who has put up with being a fishing widow all her life but has recently joined me on some trips, the two quotations on the title page are dedicated. As for the book itself, I dedicate it to my grandsons Regan and James, the next generation, and, look out everyone, maybe my granddaughter Imani too.

A List of Classic Fishing Books

By its nature, this is a personal list – if you are a big reader, you will have your own favourites and I expect we could argue for hours about what should go in and what should come out, sitting at the fireside in an angling pub, with the river fining down after a big flood and an exciting morning in prospect. I haven't put these books in any particular order, because I don't think they can be ranked and compared like that – they all have their virtues. Neither am I going to tell you what any of them are about, because that would spoil the fun that you will get from reading them.

Some of these books are out of print and can only be found through second-hand booksellers (try Coch-y-bonddu Books from the contacts list in the back). Others are still in print, thanks to specialist angling publishers like the Medlar Press. Medlar are worth a particular mention, not only because they publish good cheap editions of some real classics, but also for their other books, which cover just about every aspect of angling. And then, of course, there is the incomparable *Waterlog* magazine…

Mainly about fly fishing

Going Fishing, Negley Farson, Country Life (1942)

A Man May Fish, T. C. Kingsmill Moore, Herbert Jenkins (1960) Out of print

Where the Bright Waters Meet, Harry Plunket Greene, Philip Allan (1924) Fly Fisher's Classic Library

The Old Man and the Sea, Ernest Hemingway, Charles Scribner's (1952)

Rod & Line, Arthur Ransome, Jonathon Cape (1959)

Days and Nights of Salmon Fishing, William Scrope, John Murray (1843)

Trout Bum, John Gierach, Pruett Publishing & Co. (1986)

Fishing the Wilder Shores, Sidney Spencer, Witherby (1991)

The Habit of Rivers, Ted Leeson, Lyons and Burford, Lyons Press (1994)

A Summer on the Test, John Waller Hills, Philip Allan (1924)

Fly Fishing, Sir Edward Grey, J. M. Dent (1899)

The Well-Tempered Angler, Arnold Gingrich, Knopf (1965)

The Seven Rivers: A Lifetime of Fly Fishing in Australia and New Zealand, Douglas Stewart, Duffy and Snellgrove (1966)

A Leaf from French Eddy, Ben Hur Lampman, Touchstone Press (1965)

A Creel of Willow, N. H. Canaway, Michael Joseph (1957)

An Angler at Large, William Caine, Kegan Paul (1911)

Mainly about coarse fishing

Casting at the Sun, Chris Yates, Pelham Books (1986)

The Domesday Book of Mammoth Pike, Frederick Buller, Stanley Paul (1979)

An Open Creel, H. T. Sheringham, Methuen (1910)

At the Tail of the Weir, Patrick Chalmers, Philip Allan (1932)

The New Complete Angler, Stephen Downes, Orbis (1983)

Passion for Pike, Ad Swier, Coch-y-bonnddu Books (2006)

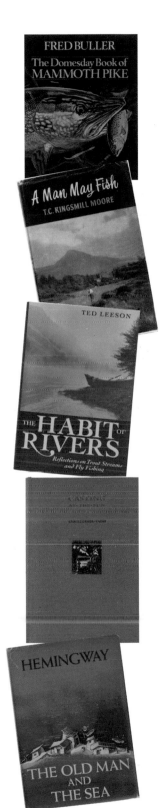

Useful Information

RETAIL

Cabela's
Nowhere else like them. Their catalogues are the business.
http://www.cabelas.com/

Sportfish
Excellent mail order supplier of game fishing gear.
http://www.sportfish.co.uk/

Farlow – of Pall Mall
Everything for the game fisherman.
http://www.farlows.co.uk/

Hardy and Grey's of Alnwick
Top class trout, salmon, coarse and sea fishing rods and reels. Probably the best known manufacturers of rods in the UK today.
http://www.greysfishing.com/

Hooked – tackle and bait
Wide selection of coarse fishing gear.
http://www.fishing-direct.com/

Kaufmann Streamborn
http://www.kaufmannsstreamborn.com/

Orvis UK
Country clothing and fly fishing kit.
http://www.orvis.co.uk/

Tackle.co.uk
Coarse, sea and game fishing mail order supplier.
http://www.tackleuk.co.uk/

Tackleshop.co.uk
Just about everything for the coarse and game angler.
http://www.tackleshop.co.uk/

The Fly Shop
In Redding, California.
http://www.flyshop.com/

BOOKS

Coch-y-bonddu Books
Probably the UK's biggest outlet for second hand sporting books – some real bargains to be had here.
http://www.anglebooks.com/

Medlar Press
The biggest UK publisher of quality angling books.
http://www.medlarpress.com/

Merlin Unwin Books
UK publisher with plenty of fishing and countryside stuff.
http://www.merlinunwin.co.uk/

MAGAZINES

Fly Fishing and Fly Tying
Good when it was first launched and has never looked back since.
http://www.flyfishing-and-flytying.co.uk/

Waterlog
A great read about every type of fishing – subscription only.
http://www.waterlogmagazine.com/

SOCIETIES

The Anglers' Conservation Association
The people who prosecute the polluters – join 'em.
http://www.a-c-a.org/

Bass Anglers' Sportfishing Society
All the news on the UK bass scene.
http://www.ukbass.com/

The Carp Society
http://www.thecarpsociety.com/

The Barbel Society
http://www.barbelsociety.co.uk/

The Fly Dressers' Guild
http://www.the-fdg.org/

TACKLE MAKERS

Abu Garcia
Two great reel makers rolled into one.
http://www.abu-garcia.com/

The Donegal Fly Fishing Company
Formed in 2001 to reintroduce high-quality fishing flies. My supplier of flies.
http://wwwdonegalfly.com/

Edward Barder Rod Company
Makers of traditional split-cane British coarse and fly rods.
http://www.barder-rod.co.uk/

Renzetti
Makers of some of the world's best fly tying vices.
http://www.renzetti.com/

Sage
World class fly rods and reels.
http://www.sageflyfish.com/

Shimano
Famous for their fixed spool reels and multipliers, but they make all kinds of other kit, too.
http://www.shimano.com/

WEBZINES AND OTHER GENERAL SITES: A SELECTION OF THE BEST

American Museum of Fly Fishing History
http://www.amff.com/

Anglers' Net
http://www.anglersnet.co.uk/

Fly Fishing History
An entertaining look at two thousand years of fluff chucking.
http://www.flyfishinghistory.com/

Global Fly Fisher
http://globalflyfisher.com/

Specialist Anglers' Alliance
The place for UK record fish claims and much else.
http://www.anglingsites.com/saa/index.htm

Vladimir Markov
Possibly the most easterly fly tyer in the world, given Vlad lives in Irkutsk, Siberia. Great guy.
http://www.markov.baikal.ru/

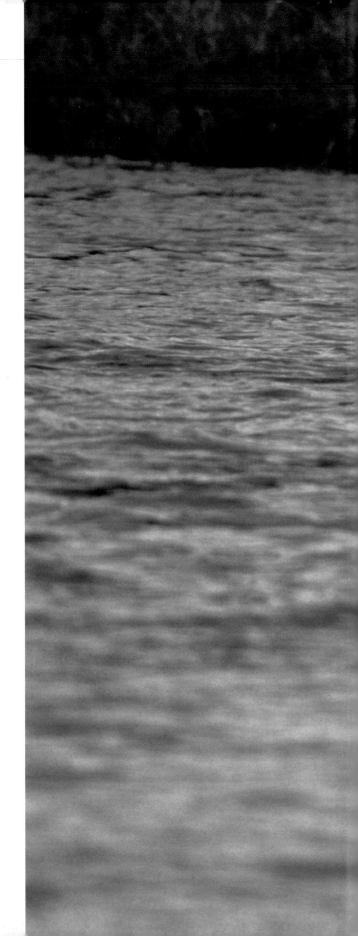

Picture credits

Every effort has been made to acknowledge the correct copyright holders as below and the publishers will, if notified, correct any errors in future editions.

Adam Wheatley 1, 131-35, 196 (top), 198 (top), 232.

Alamy Images 13, 44, 45,179, 218-19, 223.

Andrew Herd 12, 36 (bottom), 42 (top), 50, 83, 84, 85, 86, 87, 90, 112, 146, 149 (all), 150, 151, 155, 164, 165, 166-67, 178 (all), 234 (all), 235 (all), endpapers.

B & C Alexander / ArcticPhoto.com 106, 107 (top), 116, 119, 141, 170, 171.

The Bridgeman Art Library 20-1, 22, 23, 26.

Corbis 24 (bottom), 36 (top), 122 (top), 189 (bottom), 222 (top), 224 (top), 225 (all).

Don Brownlow Photography 108, 109, 120, 122 (bottom), 123.

Excellent Press, Ludlow 92-3 (From *Salmon Fishing*, Hugh Falkus, Witherby, 1984).

FotoLibrary 29 (bottom)/Nick Jenkins, 113/James Marshall, 117/Paul Carter, 118/David Brown.

Getty Images 2-3, 6-7, 9, 11, 14-15, 54 (top), 65 (bottom), 66 (all), 67 (top), 68 (all), 69 (all), 71 (top), 72 (middle and bottom), 73 (top), 74 (bottom), 76 (top), 77 (all), 89, 91, 98, 104 (all), 111 (all), 126-27, 128-29, 129, 137, 156-57, 172-73, 180 (top and bottom), 181 (bottom), 182 (top), 183 (all), 212, 215, 216 (all), 217, 220, 221 (all), 225 (top).

Ian Botham 10, 130, 174-75, 179, 192-95, 196 (bottom), 197 (all), 198 (bottom), 199-211, 233.

Jason Neuswanger / www.troutnut.com 42 (middle and bottom), 43.

Medlar Photo Library 25 (top and bottom), 27 (top and bottom), 28 (top and bottom), 29 (top), 30, 31, 32 (bottom), 33, 35 (bottom), 37, 41, 46, 48-9, 88, 110, 136, 138 (all), 139 (all), 142-43, 147, 154 (all), 158, 159 (all), 160 (all), 162 (bottom), 163 (all), 184, 185 (all), 186 (all), 187 (top), 188, 189 (top).

Museum of Fine Arts, Boston, Massachusetts, USA 24 (top).

Nature Picture Library 53 (all), 54 (bottom), 55 (all), 56, 57 (all), 58 (all), 59 (all), 60 (all), 61 (all), 62 (all), 63 (all), 65 (top), 67 (bottom), 70, 71 (middle and bottom), 72 (top), 73 (bottom), 74 (top), 75 (all), 76 (bottom), 153 (all), 168, 169, 180 (middle), 181 (top and middle), 182 (middle and bottom), 222 (top), 224 (bottom).

PA/EMPICS Photos 78-9 (David Cheskin), 107 (bottom).

Pat Walker 38 (all).

Paul Micklen / National Geographic Society 100, 101, 102-03, 105 (all).

Rex Features 161, 162 (top x 2), 187.

Shay Fennelly / www.aquaphoto.ie 190-91 (all).

Sheffield City Council, Local Studies Central Library 32 (top).

TopFoto 114.

U.S. Department of Commerce, N.O.A.A Central Library, Historic Fisheries Collection 47 (top and bottom).

Weidenfeld & Nicolson Archive 34, 35 (top), 52, 64, 81, 99, 145, 177.

Zeb Hogan, University of Nevada – Reno, USA 18, 140.

First published in Great Britain in 2008 by Weidenfeld & Nicolson

10 9 8 7 6 5 4 3 2 1

Text © Ian Botham 2008
Design and layout ©
Weidenfeld & Nicolson 2008

The right of Ian Botham to be identified as the authors of this work has been asserted in accordance with the Copyright, Designs and Patents Act 1988.

A CIP catalogue record for this book is available from the British Library.

ISBN: 978 0 297 85460 9

Colour reproduction by
DL Interactive UK
Printed and bound in Germany
by Mohn Media

Weidenfeld & Nicolson
The Orion Publishing Group Ltd
Orion House
5 Upper St Martin's Lane
London WC2H 9EA

An Hachette Livre company

The Orion Publishing Group's policy is to use papers that are natural, renewable and recyclable products and made from wood grown in sustainable forests. The logging and manufacturing processes are expected to conform to the environmental regulations of the country of origin.